Cooking the Ayurvedic Yoga Diet

Cooking the Ayurvedic Yoga Diet

A *Yoga Sutra* of Simply Healthful and Tasty Recipes

Chef Zubin D'souza
Executive Chef

YBK Publishers
New York

YBK Publishers, Inc.
39 Crosby St.
New York, NY 10013
www.ybkpublishers.com

Cooking the Ayurvedic Yoga Diet: A *Yoga Sutra* of Simply Healthful and Tasty Recipes

ISBN: 978-1-936411-30-6

Library of Congress Control Number: 2014947709

Manufactured in the United States of America,
or in the United Kingdom when distributed elsewhere.

Ver 14-08

This book is for my son, Zeus,
who inspires me
with his sense of curosity
and wonderment.

It is through him
that I have come to appreciate
the little things in life.

It is also because of him
that I feel motivated
to live a longer
and healthier life.

Contents

Desserts

About the Author

The Journey

One's mid-life crisis is a tough time to live through. It's even worse when you realize that you are at the back end of twenty-eight and your sixty-year-old father is going through it at the same time!

I needed to undertake a journey. I wanted it to be a road of self-discovery filled with spiritual enlightenment, the uncovering of hidden knowledge, and sudden bouts of total gluttony.

The more I toyed with the idea, the stronger my desire grew until it turned into an all-consuming passion that covered up even my most terrible fears. I skimped and scrounged until I had saved enough money to go off on my foray into the unknown.

My bags were packed and I was in a constant state of readiness. I wanted soon to embark on what would be the most defining moment of my life, but I just could not decide on where I wanted to go. Should it be a perilous trek through the Amazon, maybe I should volunteer for a noble cause in some godforsaken place where the ravages of war had taken its toll? After many days of mulling I finally decided to travel throughout India. There were four good reasons: it was cheaper; I speak the language; people flock here from all over the world to search for answers; and, finally, because Dorothy in *The Wizard of Oz* said, "There's no place like home."

My journey was fulfilling, enlightening, and pretty far from perilous. Although I did not encounter the tin man, a scarecrow, or a cowardly lion, I *did* meet a "saint," a yoga guru, and several wise, nearly naked sages. I discussed with them the finer aspects of the Ayurveda, an ancient traditional medical science. I debated the roles of various gods in the Hindu pantheon. I lived the yogic diet and dropped ten kilos (almost twenty-five pounds) and three inches from my waist.

Was the trip worth it? I guess you will decide this soon enough as we move along. As I don't know the answer myself, and given that I am still on the first page of this book, I will reserve my own decision for later.

The journey that you are about to embark on is mostly a cookbook because I am a trained chef and that is what I do well—cook. However, there will be times when I get carried away and I will spit out my own pearls of wisdom. Ignore them if you choose—I have been warned that they are the after-effects of a self-enlightening journey.

What is Yoga???

Simply put, yoga is what yoga does, and what it does is different things for different people.

The super-jock pumping weights at the local gym scoffs at it, referring to it as exercise for sissies. It seems that women absolutely love yoga because the instructor is usually "hot" and clad only in a loin cloth. For many yoga is a form of exercise; to others a path to spiritual conquest; and to yet others, a passing fad. Apart from those reasons, one may apply the Freudian perspective, pursue the conspiracy theory, or take the nihilistic approach.

When yoga began well more than five thousand years ago, it was meant to unify the body, the mind, and the spirit. The word "yoga" comes from the Sanskrit word "yuj" which means union or yoke. The ancient Hindus believed that they were trapped on earth in a continuous cycle of life, worldly sufferings, death, and rebirth until they achieved spiritual salvation or *Moksha*. To attain this they used yoga to try to speed up the process and find moksha in the span of a single lifetime. Generally, however, they believed that they would have to pay for their sins across a couple of lifetimes, at the least. The enormity of their sinful deeds, a term simply referred to as *Karma*, specifies the number of reincarnations or lives that a person will have to endure. While this seems far-fetched to many, believers in reincarnation will definitely support this concept.

Moksha is the ultimate aim. Moksha is a close equivalent to the concept of "salvation" as it is thought of in other religions. In the Hindu context however, it implies a conquering of the physical existence or state of the body and moving oneself onto a higher plane; a supreme level of consciousness that can transcend such realities as matter, time, space, and energy.

Acharya Patanjali, a wise sage from Gonda in Uttar Pradesh is sometimes considered the founder of yoga and was known to be a great exponent of the belief. About five thousand years ago, in a treatise called the *Yoga Sutras of Patanjali*, he documented the postures, breathing exercises, and techniques that he referred to as the route to achieving direct communion with God. His writing breaks yoga into eight different paths; each one helping the exponent to attain a higher level and ability. The initial techniques concentrate on strengthening the physical and mental attributes of the human body since it is believed that a person cannot achieve greatness when his physical being is weak and his mental faculties taken up with problems.

Purists find it difficult to separate the religious aspects of yoga from its activities. Some of the exercises include the chanting of hymns or sacred texts and the veneration of gods from the Hindu pantheon. Modern day practitioners, who can be adherents of various religious philosophies, simply omit the chanting. As Acharya Govindji, a hip, modern-day, laptop-toting, ex-financial whiz and present-day mendicant states, "Yoga is for the masses; the interpretation is not reserved merely for the teachers alone, although they do facilitate the learning process"

That sounds just about right to me. If a self-confessed foodie, couch slouch and religious cynic like me can graciously be accepted into an ashram, I see no reason why anyone would use that excuse to avoid moving toward a healthier lifestyle.

...and what may I ask, is a yogi??

The word "yogi" conjures up images of scruffy guys with flowing hair and beards, covered with soot and ash. Oops! I think I may have just described a member of the Hell's Angels. A yogi is skinnier. He does not have a booming Harley and he just kind-of hangs around in saffron robes.

My attempts at humor apart, yogis have always been a center of attention since time immemorial. To ancient Indians, they were the original rock stars. Beside the fact that they indeed had long hair and several indulged in a drag of a weed-filled pipe, they were gifted, learned, and several of them carried a message to the masses that transformed their lives for the better. Of course, when The Beatles forayed in this realm while in India on a spiritual quest, they did manage to attach a bit of chic to the otherwise generally humdrum life of the yogi.

The basic definition of a yogi is a man who practices yoga. A yogini is the female version of the term.

A yogi expects to reach a state of tranquillity after bringing his body into a balance of mind and spirit, creating harmony and equilibrium. The postures and exercises are designed to shift the energies in various parts of the body around so that they do not collect and pile up as toxins.

Ancient Indian mythology records several sages and yogis who have led extraordinarily long lives, attributed in major part to their strict ayurvedic diets and their diligent practice of yoga. There are those who claim that these myths are an over-exaggeration, but the large body of work that has been left to us make these arguments seem feeble.

Although there are several yoga exercises that anyone can perform, a qualified yoga guru (teacher) will tailor-make a program designed to provide an individual and optimized result.

You are what you eat!!!

At the risk of sounding like an advertisement for the latest brand of medication to promise relief from acidity and constipation, it is true that you become the food you eat.

At some point after a meal you may realize that certain foods get you pepped up while others tend to make you lethargic. When Ayurveda was being formulated those more-than five thousand years ago, it was likely just such an observation that prompted extensive research into the effects of diet on the human constitution.

Several buzzwords and theories floated around during the early research. Terms such as *Rajasic* and *Tamasic* (we will discuss these later) were used to describe the properties of ingredients; individuals were examined to discover the effect that different diets had on them and the results were recorded in great detail. These studies carried across several centuries, even millennia, gathering a large body of knowledge.

In the early stages it was realized that as all men are not created equal, their individual constituencies differed as well. While this may not seem like a brilliant piece of deduction, we must realize that five thousand years ago, this was considered a breakthrough discovery.

The basic principle of Ayurveda is best summarized by the statement, "Let your food be your medicine and your medicine be food." Yoga and Ayurveda are interlinked. As a healthy diet is the cornerstone of a healthier lifestyle, most yogis observe a diet that follows the basic tenets of Ayurveda, refining it to better match their individual makeup. Although this method is better suited to the rural family unit of yore, modern day city dwelling has mostly eliminated the possibility for individually customized meals to be prepared, this having been replaced by generalized healthy menu.

When these concepts were first presented to me I pictured myself sitting at the most recent burger joint I had been to, looking quite like a fattened jersey cow, right down to the brass bell around my neck. It would be necessary to get in touch with my mother to sew up a suitable perforation in the seat of my pants to allow my tail to swing freely. Things would have to change!

So what are these body constituencies???

Although the recipes in this book are not *strictly* ayurvedic, they are soundly based as they were gathered from a series of small, serious-minded country hermitages as I traveled the back roads of India. They are meant to bring you the healthfulness of the method without being made difficult by its stringencies.

It will be helpful to explain the basics of your constitution. The ancients believed that all humans were composed of five elements—air, fire, earth, water, and ether (space). Ether is also known as quintessence when it is the makeup of celestial beings. The relationship of these elements to each other differs in each individual. This individuality is called "dosha." There is no good or better type of constitution, it is simply what has been genetically programmed into the body and remains largely unaltered throughout one's lifetime. This loose definition seemed rather incredulous to me at first and I thought that my friendly old swami was having a laugh at my expense. When the old man assured me that he was extremely serious, I decided to give it a rest and listen on to what he had to say.

Ancient European medical history references the four humours made famous by Hippocrates, the father of modern-day allopathic medicine. He proclaimed that the body was governed by four types of liquids—blood, phlegm, black bile, and yellow bile; that a healthy person had these liquids in perfect proportion and harmony and an imbalance would cause illness. It was believed that these humours gave off vapors that rose up to directly affect the workings of the brain.

This concept was picked up on by several well-known heavyweights such as Immanuel Kant and Alfred Adler. Terms such as melancholic, sanguine, choleric and phlegmatic were used to describe patients who suffered from an excess of the corresponding humour.

The humors were proven wrong, but, as a concept it was not just a "made up" theory.

What Hippocrates and Galen (*Galen* Claudius Galenus) picked up on and improved was a theory believed to have originated in Mesopotamia more than two thousand years ago. In fact, what they were working with were the foundations of ayurveda which originated, you'll remember, over five thousand years ago. It was carried over by Assyrian and Mesopotamian traders like a game of "whispers," and mutated through reinterpretation over the centuries.

Quintessence (ether) as an English word is an amalgam of two Latin words: "Quinta," meaning five, and "Essentia," meaning element. The ancients believed that celestial beings were composed of a mysterious fifth element which existed in its purest form within them and as a milder, polluted, form in humans. This element is what ayurvedic texts refer to as ether or space.

To understand these elements I will begin with the concepts of tri-dosha which in ayurvedic terms is referred to as the vata—pita—kapha dosha theory.

The human body is divided into three broad classifications which are vata which combines the elements of air and ether, pita which is fire and water, and kapha, a water and earth combination. Every person has all three doshas (element combinations) present in their body. One or the other of these may appear to dominate an individual's personality and appearance. Ayurvedic theory holds that doshas affect a person's appearance, psychology, tastes and preferences, and habits. Normally, most people will maintain the dosha they are born with throughout their life. It has been noted, however, that changes of domicile, occupation, or environment may cause a temporary change in their dosha.

Each dosha is responsible for given functions in the body and each has a few sections of the body assigned to it. Balanced doshas assure the smooth functioning of all parts of the body. An excess of a dosha can manifest as a toxin build-up in the very part of the body that a dosha has charge for.

The aim of ayurvedic living and diet is to enable all three doshas to be maintained at equilibrium. Imbalanced doshas cause a build-up of toxins in parts of the body that are governed by that dosha.

Vata is governed by the properties of ether and air. It is operative in the process of movement and is thought to enable reflex actions, the movement of bodily fluids, and operation of the internal organs. Feelings of nervousness, fear, lack of energy, excitement, and anxiety are linked to this dosha. The pelvic region, thighs, large intestine, bones, skin and ears are associated with vata. Any excess build-up of vata will accumulate in those regions.

Pita is a combination of the fire and water elements. Pita is linked to metabolism and to the thought processes. It governs nutrition, digestion, clarity of understanding, and, according to some purists, the twinkle in one's eyes. Santa Claus has a surplus of pita as well as having eaten a lot of it stuffed with hummus!

The pita person is subject to anger, hate, and jealousy. Pita excesses are manifested in the stomach, sweat glands, blood, small intestine, skin, fat, and eyes.

The kapha constitution is made up of earth and water. It is the element responsible for the lubrication of joints, giving strength to tissue, and moisture in the skin. It also operates in memory and immunity. Kapha resides in the chest, throat, sinuses, mouth, stomach, head, and mucus. As my guru clearly put it plainly—anyplace you would expect to find a lot of liquid or mucus.

Attributes	Vata	Pita	Kapha
Build	Slim	Medium	Large
Weight	Less than average	Average	Overweight
Hair	Dry, brown, black, knotted, brittle, scarce	Straight, oily, blonde, grey, red, bald	Thick, curly, oily, waxy, luxuriant
Eyes	Small, sunken, dry, active, black, brown, nervous	Sharp, bright, grey, green, yellow/red, sensitive to sunlight	Big, attractive, blue, calm, inviting
Nose	Uneven shape	Long and pointed, with a red tip	Short, round, button, or pug nose
Lips	Dry, chapped, black/brown in color	Red and swollen, yellow tinge	Smooth, oily, pale
Chin	Thin and angular	Pointed and tapering	Rounded, often double-chinned
Cheeks	Wrinkled, sunken	Smooth, flat	Rounded, plump
Teeth	Buck teeth, large teeth with prominent spaces between them, thin gums	Medium sized, with soft, tender gums	Healthy, white with strong gums
Neck	Slim, long	Medium-sized	Big, with folds
Chest	Flat, sunken	Medium-sized	Expanded and round/ barrel shaped
Skin	Thin, dry, cold, rough, dark	Smooth and oily, warm, rosy	Thick and oily, cool, white, pale
Belly	Thin, flat, sunken	Medium-sized	Big, round, with folds
Navel	Small, irregular	Oval, superficial	Big, deep, round, stretched
Hips	Thin, slim	Medium-sized	Large, heavy
Joints	Crack often, small	Moderate	Large, well lubricated
Appetite	Irregular, small	Large, often has severe hunger	Follows a slow and steady rhythm

Attributes	Vata	Pita	Kapha
Digestive system	Irregular digestion, often produces gas	Quick digestion, often have a burning sensation	Takes place over a prolonged period of time, often forms mucous
Taste preferences	Sweet, sour, salty	Sweet, bitter, astringent	Bitter, pungent, astringent
Thirst	Varies	Excessive	Infrequent
Stool excretion	Often constipated	Loose stools	Thick, oily, sluggish
Physical movements	Hyperactive	Moderately paced	Slow
Mental processes	Hyperactive	Moderately paced	Slow
Faith	Variable	Extremist	Consistent
Emotional tendencies	Anxiety, fear, uncertainty	Anger, hate, jealousy	Calm, greedy for material achievement
Financial status	Poor management, spends on trifles	Spends on luxuries	Good money manager, saves well
Sleep	Poor sleeper, restless	Short duration, but sound	Deep, prolonged, difficulty waking up
Dreams	Fast-paced, fear-laden	Fiery with a lot of violence	Composed of romance, lakes, snow
Intellectual processes	Quick, but with a faulty response	Accurate responses	Slow but precise response
Memory	Good short-term, poor long-term	Distinct and good recollection	Slow and sustained memory
Speech	Tends to be rapid and unclear	Sharp and penetrating	Slow, monotonous

Kapha people tend toward attachment, greed, and, surprisingly, a calm and forgiving demeanor.

While the best method for determining your constitution is by consulting a qualified ayurvedic doctor or pulse reader. In India, there are pulse readers whose method of diagnosis involves gripping your wrist and checking the pulse. The speed and the rhythm gives the pulse reader information on how your body is functioning and a further course of treatment is prescribed based on that evaluation. The chart below will help you to determine your own constitution. Award a mark to each attribute you qualify for, and then total the three columns. It is possible that you can have two dominant constitutions, or that all three are at par.

A good ayurvedic doctor may be able to tell your constitution at a simple first glance. This was a bit distressing to me as I normally stroll about in a state of total denial. There are characteristics of the dominant constitution that lead them to the correct conclusion. Flattened chests, reddened eyes, curly or straight hair are some of the characteristics that they tend to look for to tell one if you belong to the vata, pita or kapha dosha.

While certain body types that may convey the dominance of a particular dosha, the theory only holds true for those dominated by a single dosha. Honestly, I personally would not try to guess the dosha of passers-by. This chart is merely indicative. Do not try this at home!

Food and the Gunas

"This just does not translate well into English," I complained to my dear guru. He was trying to explain to me the concept of the gunas, the attributes of food. I had signed up for this course because I was under the impression that any class that is food-oriented is an excuse to stuff yourself until you burst. Anyway, that is what I make sure of when I conduct my own cooking classes.

Not so in this case! And to make it worse, my guru had moved on to discussing the virya, vipaka, and prabhav of various foods. While these concepts are easier to understand within the Indian context and perspective, they are immensely difficult to translate across languages and cultures. Shrugging aside my remonstrations of anguish, the wise old man made as if to utter some pearls of wisdom, but I guess he must have changed his mind part way through. He began to speak, changed his expression, replaced it with a wicked smile, and said, "English is a funny language that cannot accept the translations of most concepts. Until now I haven't figured out how I can read and become well-read, and it seems I must die before being dead, but, to be *well-dead,* well, that seems to be out of the question!"

Before having my aha! moment, I probed this statement for its underlying intellect and a hidden message that would help to ease the burden of this undertaking. Finding none, I realized that either he was being sarcastic, or he was poking fun at my feeble attempt to converse in proper Sanskrit, so I decided to plod on ignoring his pranks as best I could.

Once it was established that all beings have individual constitutions that control their health, emotions, and personalities; and they, in turn, are influenced by the food they consume, it becomes a natural progression that the food must be analyzed for its hidden attributes.

It was realized then, as it is now, that the food one consumes has varying effects on our health and on our bodies. Ayurveda went a step further to create lists of foods that are beneficial or harmful. With this basic groundwork done, the effects on the temperament and the mind were observed.

Several foods were seen to produce serenity; others caused an increase in activity in the body and a heightening of the imagination, while yet others induced a sense of laziness and stupor. (Yes, it must have been that large bowl of ice cream with peanuts and pistachios, chocolate sauce, and a handful of wonderful maraschino cherries.) Obviously if you have read this far into this book, you have concluded that I lived then on a diet of food that did not include any of that serenity stuff.

Satvic foods are fresh, juicy, ripe, and flavorful with a pleasant fragrance. They lead our minds to a sense of balance, purity, and awareness. These foods are fruits and vegetables, nuts, grains, sprouts, and fresh dairy products. They are the foods most eaten by yogis and those on a spiritual quest, and they are often prescribed for widows for the rest of their lives, because the teachings say that other forms of food may promote carnal desires and lust. They have a calming effect on the body and mind. Satvic diets do not include onions or garlic because they promote carnal lust and can distract a person's meditation (although some sages will have them in smaller quantities for their underlying health benefits—yeah, sher!).

Rajasic guna is usually associated with bitter, sour, salty, pungent, hot or dry food. These foods excite the mind and lead us to a state of dynamism and activity. These are the foods that lead us to acquire new things and become materialistic. This is especially true in the case of fried food and those tasty foods that cause us to overeat. While they are not the ideal foods for a yogi, they are recommended for those setting up new adventures or new business ventures.

Tamasic guna describes food that is old, unpalatable or decayed. Cold leftovers are a classic example of this type. Tamasic foods dull the senses and slow ones reactions, leading us to a state of mental inertia and ignorance (inebriation and foolishness is more like it). Ayurveda terms these as the worst kinds of foods and deems them to be avoided at all costs. Meat, fish, eggs, and alcohol fall into this category.

Well, that's what ayurveda says, but they may alter their conclusions once they see how my friends move and react to alcohol at our office parties!

Cooking ayurvedic foods is linked to the six tastes—bitter, sweet, sour, pungent, salty, and astringent. According to practitioners of ayurveda, a balance of these tastes creates healthier food. Sweet foods are meant to enhance body tissue activity, while pungent foods like chilli and ginger enhance metabolism. Astringent and bitter ingredients, like cumin and turmeric, detoxify the body and improve the immune system. Sour ingredients help to balance the acids in our body, while salt balances minerals.

While ayurveda is a complicated science and only a qualified practitioner should suggest the perfect diet that your constitution requires, you would do well to always eat foods that make your life healthier. The definition of health can be subjective. Being healthy does not mean that you must have rippling muscles and perfect pallor. Internal health is what is important— proper and ideally functioning bodily organs that do not place undue stress one's functioning. A vegetarian diet can lead you to just that state.

A hermit's life

Life in a hermitage is not so tough. You simply wake up real early, bathe in ice-cold water, pray to several deities, perform penance (sometimes this includes self-flagellation), do chores, until the fields, cook food, exercise, forage for roots, berries and herbs, pray some more, meditate, exercise, cook food again and drop off to sleep without managing to finish your meal. These activities are a total breeze for someone with incredible stamina, steely determination, and an iron resolve. Does anyone see *me* in that description?

One of my greatest understandings has been to come to learn that mediocrity in one's culinary skills is unwelcome. When there is a scarcity of food, and the purpose of a meal is only to satisfy hunger, even then the quality, freshness, and taste of one's meals are of paramount importance.

Freshness is a term that takes on new meaning when you consider a meal in a hermitage. The vegetables and milk are straight from the field with no taint of fertilizers, hormones, chemicals, lead, melamine, or other additives. Honey is right from the beehives after carefully being sure that none of the bees are harmed and they are successfully relocated during the process. Sugar is produced from freshly pressed cane juice. Wild berries are picked and served (and some munched off the plant), the remainder stored in clay- and cow-dung plastered rooms to be later turned into syrups or dried. Grains are harvested, husked manually, and ground on stone mills, which preserves a great deal of its flavor.

Every step taken is with a view of advancing one's spiritual as well as physical well-being. I have never seen so many people content with so very little. Money has little use in the community. Debts are paid by returning favors or setting aside time to assist one's benefactors with their chores. Electricity doesn't exist and time and weather is determined and regulated by the observance of the sun, celestial bodies, and the activities of the animals.

I went into this with a romantic notion of what life would be like within the confines of this alien world, so nothing prepared me for my initial days. I had earlier pictured myself as a sobered-down Steven Seagal or a Rambo working on some metal while monks went about me with serene faces and a prayer on their lips. It is a rude awakening that your Blackberry does not find a network and you cannot recharge your laptop. But, when you allow yourself to ease into that life and become immersed in the calm, it brings one to a feeling of being at one with your soul and the universe. I know that that sounds trite and you've read it before, but it is a feeling that I find truly difficult to recreate in the stress-filled, smoky kitchens that are my regular world. There is no doubt that I felt out of kilter in those villages and hermitages, responding to a feeling that I did belong, but really did not, prompting my decision to return to the decaying, materialistic world that I am so much in sync with.

That I could not stay is not the response of everyone, nor does it prove that it is a difficult transition. It was simply *my* response. I have watched people from far more complex backgrounds melt easily into this uncomplicated society. I cannot envy their ability to blend and easily cross the barriers that divide, but I do envy that, for them, for right now, they appear to be living the simple life we seem all to crave.

Basic yoga exercises

Of what use is an ayurvedic diet without some yoga to back it up?! Yes, there are the complicated back twists, headstands, and every unbelievable contortion that you can think of, but do we really want to do that? If your answer is yes, then you must have a professional guide or you might end up with a broken neck. A professional teacher is of great advantage because yoga is a science that one does not innovate upon. It is something that one learns in a prescribed manner that was laid out several thousand years ago.

Yoga will give you flexibility, a rejuvenated and better-functioning system and a healthy, glowing body. I can vouch for the glow because all those headstands have given me a nice, shiny skull where hair has since declined to grow!

The Indian Kitchen

In a country suffering from obesity, cardiac arrest, diabetes and other gluttony related diseases, you have to believe that many Indians take their food habits very, very seriously. The United States has similar problems, but, except for a few politicians, has not yet come to recognize what the result of this will be.

India is populated by many who are almost fanatical about the food they eat and how they maintain their kitchen. Several religious diktats, superstitions, and social/cultural customs dictate how a kitchen is to be kept.

In the past, the family cook, the matriarch of the house, kept strict vigil over what was considered to be a personal fiefdom. Those who trespassed or violated the code were severely dealt with. Punishments might include peeling bushels of spicy red onions or winnowing the wheat to separate the chaff from the grains. Nowadays, that prepared food has become so available, the punishments, even so, have kept pace so as to ensure that offenses are never repeated.

The reason that the kitchen has been accorded such high status is because they are considered to be the equivalent of a holy temple. Rules similar to those that apply when visiting a temple are maintained. Shoes and footwear are never worn and the sanctum sanctorum is open only to members of the family. Visitors are frequently barred from entering the kitchen.

Personally, I am partial to the way the Bengali community treats their kitchen. Apart from following the basic "no shoes," the matriarch does the honors each day. After a refreshing cold-water bath and the mandatory daily prayers, the chanting of sacred verses, and the singing of hymns, the mother puts a vermillion and sandalwood *tilak* on her forehead and enters the kitchen. The windows are opened to let in the sunlight and fresh morning air that drives off the stale smell of the previous day. The windows are kept shut at night to prevent the entry of scavenging animals. A pot of water is put to boil to brew the first cups of tea for the family. Most Indians live for this moment, to have a cup of tea served to them as soon as they wake up, just as Americans must have their first cup of coffee. That out of the way, the kitchen then sees great activity with the preparation of all of the remaining meals that are spaced evenly throughout the day to be sure that we get our full five square meals. Huge pots of hot water are employed to clean up the place in between cooking sessions. It is something that is best experienced firsthand, but I warn you, if you get caught having a peek, be prepared to peel at least a hundred pounds of onions.

Ghee

In India, there is a saying that translates to mean that ghee (clarified butter) provides one more benefit than one's parents and the entire medical community together. In India, ghee has a long history.

Originally thought to be gotten around 2000 B.C. from the Aryans, who were nomadic herdsmen, ghee made its way into several sacred Vedic texts and hymns, including the famous *Mahabharata.* It is used as a sacrifice during several Hindu ceremonies and is considered to be one fifth of the foods that gave the gods their immortality. Ghee holds a position of great significance in the Ayurveda, even as it is practiced to this day.

Ghee is a pure fat, clarified butter from which the milk solids and water have been removed. It has a shelf life at room temperature that far outlasts butter and can be stored in an airtight container for a couple of months. It is a common product which is available in some supermarkets and all Indian provision stores around the globe. It is easily prepared at home using store-bought butter.

Traditionally, ghee is prepared from home-churned butter, and although difficult to procure, ghee simmered in clay pots over wood fires has a beautiful smokiness. Its fragrance is pronounced, and it can really make a difference to a recipe. However this smoked version is usually made by farmers for their own consumption and they become a tad irritated should they see someone try to make off with any of their precious store. It is best that I should provide you with the method to make your own ghee from butter.

Using a microwave is easiest. Place a pound of room temperature unsalted butter into a deep microwaveable bowl and cover it with plastic wrap. Setting it to medium should be enough to ensure that the water has evaporated from the liquid and the fat has separated from the milk solids that sink to the bottom. Gently spoon off and reserve the clear liquid ghee at the top without disturbing the milk solids at the bottom. This can be stored in an airtight container.

The pan-on-the-stove method requires a bit of patience and practice. Place a pound of soft, unsalted butter in a heavy-bottomed pan and simmer gently for about ten minutes until the liquid begins to froth. Increase the flame gradually until the liquid bubbles and then reduce it to a simmer once again. Skim off and throw away the froth that rises to the top. When the butter appears clear and you can see flecks of golden solids at the bottom, it is done. Remove it from the flame and pour it off carefully in order to avoid mixing in the solids.

Spices and herbs found in a yogi's kitchen

Spices have been used in India for several thousands of years. They were originally used for their medicinal properties and to mask the flavor of food that has gone off. The listing of these herbs and spices, while naming the bodily organs they are thought to affect, and stating their use as remedies, is historical and is neither proposed for nor intended for medicinal use.

Cinnamon/ Dalchini The thin rolled bark of an evergreen tree. It is often confused with the cassia bark that comes from China. You can buy the flattened or rolled bark in most Asian stores or supermarkets. I tend to avoid the powdered option since a major part of the flavor missing is missing. Cinnamon has been used in various remedies for stomach ailments and as a calming tea.

Cumin/Jeera is a member of the parsley family. It is a pretty plant that sprouts clusters of white and pink flowers. The seeds are used to season food. It is found in three colors; white, black, and amber. The black seeds are the ones most commonly found in the Indian markets.

Ayurveda uses it in remedies to treat digestive problems caused by overeating. It can be chewed or made into a tea to dispel symptoms of colitis, gas, and abdominal pain.

Cardamom pods/Chota elaichi grows on a perennial bush that is between six and ten feet high. It is highly sought after for its rich fragrance and distinctive flavor.

It is among the most expensive spices in the world. The reason for its expense is that each pod is harvested by hand.

In Indian homes it is used as a mouth freshener after a meal. It is often found for the taking in a bowl at Indian restaurants in the United States near to the door as you exit.

According to ayurveda, it helps the spleen and pancreas in the absorption of nutrients, and it helps to digest food in the colon.

Fenugreek/Methi seeds are known throughout India. It is used a great deal in Bengali and South Indian cuisine.

This spice provides edible leaves and shoots that are used in a wide variety of Indian foods from salads to sweets.
It has been used to treat diabetes, allergies, bronchitis, flu and dysentery.

Curry leaves/kadi patta It is through a misinterpretation of the native name of these leaves kariveppilai that the word curry came about. The leaves may be used fresh or dried, but an Indian home might have a curry leaf tree growing in the backyard to provide an unending supply of this amazing flavor.

The leaves are often used as a poultice or in one's bath water to help ward off body lice and skin ailments.

Carom seeds/bishop's weed/ajwain These resemble a smaller version of caraway seeds. They have a unique sharp and pungent flavor. It is often used in to enhance the flavor of certain types of dough or bland vegetables.

It has been used to relieve problems of indigestion and colitis.

Black cardamom pods/ badi elaichi are distinctly different from the fragrant green pods. They are often used with other spices to create a garam masala mix. It is normally used whole to season heavily flavored curries and some sweetmeats.

Asafoetida/hing One of its names, "Devil's Dung," projects the fragrance of this gummy resin-like substance that is extracted from the dill plant. It is available in powdered or whole form. It imparts a strong almost sulphur-like fragrance. When cooked, its flavor almost replicates that of a combination of cooked ginger and garlic and is used when diets require these two bulbs to be eliminated. When using the whole form, dissolve it in a bit of water.

It was used by singers as a throat gargle in ancient times. More recently it was used to cure stomach ailments that arise from overeating.

Coriander seeds/coriander leaves/Dhaniya Coriander seeds are grouped under spices and its leaves under herbs. They have separate fragrances and flavors.

Coriander seeds can be brewed into a tea for stomach ailments or used as a diuretic. When soaked in water overnight, the liquid has been used as an eyewash.

Coriander leaves are considered an aphrodisiac and its juice has been used as an antihistamine.

Fennel seeds/ Saunf Although the fennel bulb is not often used in Indian cooking, the seeds are. Their sweetish fragrance and the flavor they impart, complements several vegetables when they are stir-fried. Fennel is often used as a mouth freshener after meals and it is used sometimes to lend fragrance to desserts.

Fennel has been known to relieve the the symptoms of abdominal pain, colic and vomiting, weakness of vision, and menstrual cramps.

Turmeric/ Haldi This rhizome is cultivated in most parts of India and is among the most widely used spices in Indian cooking. It is included in almost every preparation and in every region.

One reason for its widespread use is because of its potency as an antiseptic. It can render safe most food that has not been stored under refrigeration and on the border of spoiling.

It is used widely as an antiseptic for cuts, and as a face and body pack to rid the skin of blemishes. This use is so popular that a ceremony is carried out on the day before most Indian weddings when family and friends smear the bride and the groom with turmeric paste so that their skin is at its best for the wedding day.

Turmeric is also said to be helpful in treating urinary diseases and to relieve body ache.

Black peppercorns/kali mirch are grown mostly in Kerala. At one time they were so expensive that they were worth almost their weight in gold. At that time, part of one's salary might be paid in the cloves and peppercorns.

Peppercorns have traditionally been used to relieve the symptoms of colds, coughs, and sore throats.

Dried Red Chillies/Sukha Lal Mirch are available all over India, ranging from mild Kashmiri chillies to the chart-busting Naga chillies. They are dried and ground to flakes for sprinkling or into a fine powder for seasoning food. They are often used whole in tempering.

Although ayurveda maintains that dried red chillies are more harmful than the fresh green ones when consumed, they are sometimes made into a pain reliever when slowly steeped in warm oil. That oil is then massaged into the body.

Saffron/ Zaffran/Kesar Saffron is the most expensive flavoring in the world. Saffron strands are the dried stigma of the crocus flower. Each crocus flower has only three pistils which must be picked by hand and the saffron then manually extracted. About ten thousand blooms are required to extract a kilo of saffron. Saffron imparts a beautiful orange color when it is dissolved. Dissolving it in a bit of warm milk gives the best results. The lactic acid in the milk helps to release the flavor.

Cloves/Laung Black peppercorns and cloves were the spices in demand in ancient times. Wars were fought to establish supremacy in the shipping routes to South India for the trade in these spices. Cloves provide a sharp astringent flavor.
The whole spice as well as an oil extract have been traditional remedies for toothaches and cavities.

Poppy seeds/Khus Khus Poppy seeds impart a nutty taste to foods. They are first soaked in water before grinding them into a paste. Its raw flavor must first be cooked out before it can be used.

It has a mild sedative effect.

Chaat Masala This is a readymade product available at most Indian groceries. It is tangy sprinkle that is a combination of spices and dry mango powder. It is sprinkled over kebabs, chaats, and salads. It is sometimes used on fruits or fruit salads to give it a tangy, savory zing.

Roasting spices for making roasted spice powder

This dry roasting method gives an enhanced flavor to spices that are prepared to sprinkle over foods when the roasting of whole spices is not part of the recipe. Individual spices are roasted in an extremely hot griddle pan until they begin to change colour. The spices are then ground in a food processor or pounded using a mortar and pestle.

Spices commonly converted to roast spice powders are cumin, fennel, coriander, cinnamon, and cardamom. These self-prepared powders have greater flavor than do commercially prepared powdered spices.

Basic Kitchen Equipment

Though the preparation of most Indian meals does not require special equipment, a collection of a few of the items discussed in this section will definitely help to facilitate your procedures. Indeed, many kitchens will already contain many of them.

Part of a chef's training is to be asked the hypothetical question, "What would you take with you to be stranded on a deserted island?" I've come up with a brief list of devices that are near necessities.

Food Processor This is one of those basic machines that every kitchen should have for any kind of cookery. Many Indian recipes call for ground pastes or ground spices. You can find basic grinders right up to more complicated electric all-in-one food processing units. While some of the recipes suggest grinding spices in a food processor, small amounts of spices will get lost and not be properly ground in a full-sized processor. A smaller processor or a spice grinder will do better.

Muscle is sometimes an issue. Grinding pastes in a simple home bar blender can place an immense strain on the motor causing it to burn out. An effective and efficient alternative (with the added benefit of healthful exercise) is the simple mortar and pestle.

Mortar and pestle This is a great piece of kitchen equipment that manages to simultaneously replace the food processor and a visit to the gym. Taking every opportunity to be green, several energy conservationists I know totally reject the motorized practicality of food processors in favor of the mortar and pestle. I prefer those made of stone to the lighter wooden versions. Stone washes off easier and does not absorb flavors as wood will.

Heavy-bottomed pot/Handi Many of my recipes call for the use of a heavy-bottomed pot. The purpose of the thick bottom is that Indian food is often simmered or stewed for long periods of time. There is greater chance for the spices to stick to the bottom and burn. To minimize this, use a heavy-bottomed pot; it distributes the heat more evenly and lessens heat concentration at the center of the pot. A short, squat pot with a mouth slightly wider than its base is preferable to the tall and slimmer stockpot types.

Heavy, round-bottomed wok/Kadhai This is a versatile item in Indian culinary preparation. They are filled with oil for deep-frying food. Thinner versions are used for rapid stir-frying while heavier ones made of thicker metal are used to prepare vegetable stews and curries.

Deep sauté pan This is a piece of equipment that pleases me for its multi-functionality. The high sidewalls and flat surface make it admirably suited to preparing small quantities of curry, can be filled with oil to replicate a deep-fat fryer, and can be used to dry-roast spices before grinding them.

Griddle plate or griddle pan/Tava With so many advances in technology, grandma's original cast-iron pans have been almost replaced, but I understand that, among devotees, such a statement is almost irreligious. Griddles are perfect for baking unleavened bread, sear-frying kebabs and cutlets, and do a pretty good job of replicating the baking normally resultant of a tandoor oven.

Rolling Pin This is a true necessity if breads are going to be a part of your meal. It's probable that your kitchen already has one and it's likely to be wooden; most Indians prefer the wooden ones. When rolling out a dozen or more breads all you need is a sturdy pin that is comfortable for you to use. Heavier rolling pins do a good job of crushing spices and cracking nuts as well.

* * *

Note: Indian food processors have a special attachment, a tiny jar, like a coffee grinder, with which we grind our spices. I've checked and found that these attachments are not easily available in the U.S. If a fortunate reader should happen upon an equivalent device available in the U.S., please let our other readers know this by writing to me at zubin@chefzubin.com. I will pass the word along on our website: www.chefzubin.com.

Basic preparations

While I expect that many readers will be familiar with cookery in general and the basic preparations required for Indian cooking, there are those who are venturing into this brave new world for the first time. Allow me to guide you through a few of the terms and basic Indian preparations.

Coconut Milk

The fast and easy out is canned or powdered. Canned coconut milk is available in almost all general food stores. Good, perhaps, but for the sake of the many food elite who would scoff at the notion of canned coconut milk in their curries, here are the two best methods to get at those raspy little rascals:

Your Own Coconut Milk Extracted from Brown Coconuts

The brown outer shell of the coconut is discarded. (In fact, the hairy outer husk, called "coir," is used to make rope.) The brown coating/skin on the surface of the coconut kernel may be ground with the coconut meat though some claim that it changes the color of the milk and they peel it off. Peeling it or not makes no difference to the curries appearing in this book.

After removing the hard external shell, the flesh is cut into manageable pieces and ground in a food processor with a bit of water to facilitate the process.

The thick mixture that results is squeezed through a single layer of cheese cloth. This first extraction is known as thick coconut milk. The coconut flesh can then be returned to the food processor to be ground again with more water. The resultant liquid when squeezed through a cheese cloth is thin coconut milk.

Fresh coconut milk tends to curdle when it is boiled for a long period of time or when it is put into an acidic medium so the cooking process begins with thin coconut milk and is finished off and thickened with the first extraction, the thick coconut milk.

Frankly, authenticity apart, and with a deferent bow to the "slow food movement," I recommend cracking open a can of coconut milk (but not with your mortar and pestle). Canned coconut milk of Thai origin, Maggi coconut milk powder [I've never seen this in the U.S., ed.], and commercially available UHT (ultra heat treated) coconut milk are great substitutes for the coconut extraction process. If you use any of these products, there is no need to concern yourself about first/second extract or thin/thick coconut milk. Just use the product directly as there is little chance of these products curdling.

Coconut Milk from Desiccated Coconut

In areas where fresh coconut is not readily available, desiccated coconut may be used. The method is similar. Place the desiccated coconut in a bowl and cover with hot water. Allow it to reconstitute for ten to fifteen minutes and then process in a food processor. Squeeze the milk out through cheese cloth, following the instructions for fresh coconut above.

Tamarind

Tamarind is available in many forms though the treatment to achieve the use of the pulp remains similar.

Tamarind cakes are a deseeded and compressed version of the fruit. During manufacturing the fruit is processed whole, the seeds are removed, and it is then simply pressed together.

Dried tamarind is the fresh fruit that has been sun-dried.

All one does is place the tamarind—fresh, cakes, or dried—into a pot, cover with water and simmer for about twenty minutes. You will see a thick pulp begin to form. Remove from the heat and set it aside to cool. Pass the pulp through a sieve, discarding the fibrous remnants and use the sieved pulp as needed. It can be stored refrigerated, in an air-tight jar, for something on the order of a couple of months.

Panch-Phoran—How To Make It

This is a term used for a mixture of five spices, used predominantly in the cooking of the states of Bengal, Bihar and Orissa. This mixture is often referred to as Indian five-spice and is usually prepared in quantity at home and stored for later use.

A very simple method, making it involves mixing together equal quantities of fenugreek seeds, cumin seeds, fennel seeds, mustard seeds and onion seeds. When used, a pinch of the mixture is thrown into hot oil. When the spices crackle and release their aroma, the remainder of the dish's ingredients are added as per the recipe being followed.

Panch Phoran gives a finished dish a complex mélange of flavors. However, this mix does not lend itself easily to experimentation. It is best used within the confines of prescribed recipes.

How to Chop Onions
Without Adding the Salt of One's Tears

Legend has it that a delegation of onions went to petition Lord Brahma, the Hindu god of creation. They stated that they do gladly sacrifice their lives to enhance the palatability of humankind's meals yet they receive no thanks nor even brief mention. Invoking his divine powers and grace, Lord Brahma granted them great favor by proclaiming that whosoever shall cut onions from that day on would weep with pain in the memory of their slain brethren.

A touching story! However, it has done absolutely nothing to slack the tide of self-proclaimed experts who dish out their secret recipes to combat this effect. In my many years as a chef, I have witnessed numerous "cures" that range from the possibly believable to the flat-out bizarre.

Many believe in the power of a slice of bread held between one's teeth while chopping the onions. I was once even offered the suggestion that the bread should be buttered!

Indian kitchens call for great amounts of chopped onions to be used as a base for any of several curries, as a thickener, or as a filler. Onions, tasting wonderful when cooked, and being one of the cheapest vegetables at the market, they quickly gained a place of great use in many recipes—because they add flavor and deliver satiety at an economical price.

Indians prefer using sharp red onions to their milder flavored white cousins because they have less moisture and caramelize faster and because, in India, they are cheaper. In the U.S., red onions are commonly called Spanish onions, and the reverse is true; white onions caramelize more readily than red, and they are often cheaper.

What to do? You are faced with a basket full of onions requiring peeling and chopping. The easiest way to prevent crying yourself is to delegate the job to someone else. If your position in the home hierarchy grants no such privilege make sure that you are in a well ventilated area.

Always use a sharp knife to peel and cut. Onion cells contain a sulphur-based acid that is released into the air when cells are ruptured or broken. A sharp knife will cut more cleanly through the cell and allow less release of the juices containing the irritant to squirt all about. Placing the onions in a bowl of water after peeling them and quickly trashing the peels also tends to help a bit.

And now for something completely different. If my plan fails you are welcome to try a method that my pal Vishal swears by. He claims to have never cried while slicing onions because he keeps an onion circle tucked on his left ear. He hasn't yet figured out how to get his wife, Saloni, to ignore the smell that lingers into the evening!

How To Cook Onions

Onions have been around for more than five thousand years. Ancient Vedic texts mention them, as do Sumerian writings, ancient Egyptian scrolls, and there is a brief mention in the Biblical book of Numbers.

Onions were originally believed to have mystical properties. The great Indian physician Charaka (c. 300 B.C.E.) mentions their antiseptic properties as well as their diuretic capabilities. The ancient Egyptians invested this humble vegetable with revered mystical qualities, interpreting its circle within a circle structure to represent infinity. They used onion in their mummification process in the hope that the dead would find them useful in the afterlife.

Some societies in ancient India banned the consumption of onions or garlic to widows, celibates, and sages because the carnal lust onions promote would cause the loss of status or concentration during meditation.

Onions were used in the treatment of cholera and thought to slake the patient's thirst.

Given that basic trivia about onions, what do they really do? They can be pickled rather easily They can be dried so they keep for long periods of time. But, most importantly, they are vital to Indian cookery.

In India, onions are among the cheapest vegetables one can obtain. Since economics is often a prime factor in the consideration of diet and many vegetables prove expensive to a significant portion of the population, large quantities of onions were used to bulk up meals. When cooked, onions are a great thickener and they impart a characteristic sweetness that helps to balance other tastes in the dish.

Indians take the browning of their onions seriously. Traditionally a lot of oil is used to ensure that the onions are well browned which in turn results in the final product having a distinct oily feel to it, but the rich flavor of the carmelization caused by frying them brown is what's important.

When onions are immersed in oil at high heat, moisture from the onions evaporates rapidly and the onions brown faster and more evenly. Some Indians deep fry sliced onions until they are golden and crisp before grinding them.

Most dishes call for onions to be cooked until they are golden brown. Care must be taken because there is a fine line dividing desirable golden brown from acrid "golden" black. Simmering the onions while occasionally stirring them is the best way to ensure that they are cooked to perfection. I prefer a copper pot or a non-stick casserole. Stainless steel heats faster and causes the onions to stick and burn if they are not carefully watched. A convenient but not so healthy option (if you have a deep cooker always at the ready) has some chefs separately deep fry the onions until they are golden, processing them to a paste. They use this in curries to eliminate their diners coming across partially cooked onions—which among Indians is equivalent to culinary heresy.

How to Make Ginger Paste

Grind peeled ginger in a food processor with an amount of water that will result in a paste. Indian provision stores carry pre-packaged ginger paste or you can use finely chopped ginger as a substitute.

How to Store Fresh Herbs

Coriander leaves, fresh mint and dill leaves are three herbs often used in Indian cuisine. Storing them so they retain their vitality is of great importance, especially in areas where they are not easy to obtain fresh.

The best method I have come across is to cut off the roots, place the herbs stem first into a bowl of steaming hot water so that they are immersed halfway up their shoots and then place the entire lot into a refrigerator. Herbs tend to stay fresh for about ten days this way. Whenever you find your herbs drooping, discard the old water and repeat the process.

While that is the best method, if you don't have enough space in your refrigerator, wash the herbs well, flick them hard in the air to release the water trapped between the leaves, roll them in two sheets of kitchen paper toweling, enclose them in a plastic bag and refrigerate. In this manner they should stay fresh for about a week.

Another method for keeping some greens longer is similar. Do not rinse. Leave the roots on when they are present and wrap the bottoms of the stalks of leafy greens only high enough to get a grasp, in a sheet of wetted (but not dripping) paper toweling. Put them in a plastic bag with a twist tie at the top, evacuating as much air as possible by compressing, or use a plastic straw stuck through the turns of the plastic bag before it is tied, to suck out as much air as possible. I've had coriander keep this way for nearly a month.

The Cooking of Spices

Indians use both whole and ground spices in their food preparation. The whole spices used most usually are cumin, cinnamon, cardamom, and cloves; the ground spices used most usually are chilli, turmeric and coriander powders.

Many recipes begin with the rapid and brief heating of whole spices in hot oil or ghee while ground spices are brought into the recipe at a later stage as they have a tendency to stick to the bottom and burn.

Adding whole spices to hot fat cause them to swell, crackle, and turn golden, releasing their flavor to the oil and their aroma to the air. This is the ideal time to immediately begin the next stage of the recipe. If the spices are allowed to heat for longer, they will burn and spread a bitter taste to the entire dish.

To avoid concentrating powdered spices, thus allowing them to be more easily incorporated into thick sauces in preparation, mix powdered spices with a bit of water to form a paste, only then adding it to the pot.

Roasting spices before pounding them to a powder helps to enhance their fragrance and aroma. Add the spices individually to a hot, heavy, dry pan until they begin to change color. Then grind them to a powder or pulverize them using a mortar and pestle.

Much as the French technique for preparing a roux requires slow, steady heat, when powdered spices are added one must continually stir them at a simmer for five minutes or more. This enables the raw flavor of the spice to cook out. Should one fail to do this, the finished dish will have overtones of the raw spice.

The Art of Tempering

Unlike the rapid heating of whole spices, tempering is the traditional Indian process of simmering oil or ghee with spices to impart their flavor to the oil. This flavored oil is then added to the finished dish just prior to serving, thus enhancing the flavors and adding complexity.

You may continue the practice of budding chefs, who have over several centuries experimented with the spices and the amounts used in tempering the oil, thereby occasionally introducing to the cuisine over time, astounding new results.

Ancient medical treatises document the work of physicians who prescribed spice-infused oils for their therapeutic value as massage mediums to relieve pain. In a natural progression people began to ingest these oils in order to obtain their maximum result. It was not a great leap to impart this wonderful mélange and complexity of flavor to spice up a dish thus gaining immediate culinary recognition and acceptance.

The spice mixture used in the tempering process is a clear indication of the region of India from which a dish hails. The spices and other ingredients that are added will vary somewhat depending on the season or the experimental nature of the person preparing the meal. It's likely, for example, that a recipe from the southern states will include at least a few grains of lentils in the tempering. This imparts a nuttiness to the result

Regardless of the known health hazards, most Indians love to see a gleaming layer of oil spread across the stuff we intend to eat. One doesn't really need much oil to impart flavor and zing to a dish. The north seems to prefer ghee, the central and eastern regions like mustard oil, and the southern areas lean toward coconut oil. The basic methods of tempering, however, remain the same. A rule-of-thumb recipe for basic tempering follows.

For each 400 g/2 cups of a finished dish such as lentils and sauces you will need:

Oil or ghee (I prefer ghee most of the time)	30 g/1½ tbsp
Cumin seeds	3 g/½ tsp
Fresh chillies, chopped	10 g

Heat the oil and add the cumin seeds. When they crackle, add the fresh chillies and simmer for a few minutes. Pour this mixture over the dish to be tempered and stir it in to blend the flavors.

Weights and Measurements

Being Indian, I normally use the metric system. Although I have tried really hard to use that "other" form of measurement, I have failed miserably. I always have to use a conversion guide to do the calculations for me.

It has happened that a wonderful recipe failed because I was searching for my conversion chart while the onions burned merrily away. So, to avoid that, my trusty conversion chart follows.

Most of the recipes in this book have been calculated to serve four. It presumes that a single dish will not constitute the entire meal and one is also served rice or bread.

Equivalent Measures

3 teaspoons = 1 tablespoon
4 tablespoons = 1/4 cup
5 tablespoons + 1 teaspoon = 1/3 cup
8 tablespoons = 1/2 cup
12 tablespoons = 3/4 cup
16 tablespoons = 1 cup (8 ounces)
2 cups = 1 pint (16 ounces)
4 cups (2 pints) = 1 quart (32 ounces)
8 cups (4 pints) = 1/2 gallon (64 ounces)
4 quarts = 1 gallon (128 ounces)

U.S–Metric Conversion

U.S.UNITS	METRIC
1/4 teaspoon	1 ml
1/2 teaspoon	2 ml
1 teaspoon	5 ml
1 tablespoon	15 ml
1/4 cup	50 ml

U.S.UNITS	METRIC
1/3 cup	75 ml
1/2 cup	125 ml
2/3 cup	150 ml
3/4 cup	175 ml
1 cup	250 ml
1 quart	1 litre
1 ounce (oz.)	40 g/ 2 heaping tablespoons
2 ounces (oz.)	55 g/ ¼ cup
3 ounces (oz.)	85 g/ ½ cup loosely packed
4 ounces (1/4 pound)	120 g/ 5/8 cup
8 ounces (1/2 pound)	225 g/1 cup
16 ounces (1 pound)	455 g/ 2 ¼ cups

Oven Temperature Conversion and Equivalents

°F	Gas Mark/Regulo	°C
225	1/4	110
250	1/2	120
275	1	140
300	2	150
325	3	160
350	4	175
375	5	190
400	6	204
425	7	220
450	8	230
475	9	240
500	10	260

Indian Names of Commonly Used ingredients

The table on the next few pages will help you find your ingredients either locally, through the Internet, or in Asian food stores. The table shows the Indian and English equivalent names for various ingredients

The naming of items, their transliteration from a language that uses a different letter set, can create confusion and prompts the same thing to be spelled in different ways. When an ingredient may have different names through usage, I try to point this out by direct reference or by simply using the names spelled in their different ways. Thus these may appear to be spelling errors, but they are, in fact, not.

It is a common bookmaking practice to italicize "foreign" words. As this book, though written in English, is actually an Indian work, it does not treat Hindi and other Indian languages as foreign. Should I use a non English word that is not Indian, then it will be italicized. *Avanti!*

	HINDI	**ENGLISH**
MILK PRODUCTS	Paneer	Cheese
	Dahi	Yogurt
	ghee	Clarified butter
	Khoya	Reduced milk cakes
	Kheer	Rice pudding
CEREALS	Atta	Whole wheat flour
	Chawal	Rice
	Chawal atta	Rice flour
	Chira, poha	Flattened or beaten rice
	Maida	Refined wheat flour
	Moori, Murmura	Puffed rice (not to be confused with breakfast cereal)
	Seviyan	Vermicelli
	Ushna Chawal	Parboiled rice
	Sooji/Rawa	Semolina
LENTILS (DAL)	Toor/toovar dal	Split pigeon peas
	Besan	Chickpea flour
	Bori	Small sun dried cones of lentil paste
	Kabuli chana	Chickpeas, garbanzo beans
	Chana dal	Bengal gram (split chickpeas, without their seedcoat)
	Urad dal	Split black gram
	Matar dal	Yellow split peas
	Moong dal	Moong beans or green gram
	Masoor dal	Red lentil
	Papad	Poppadum
VEGETABLES	Aloo	Potato
	Bundh gobi	Cabbage
	Baigan	Brinjal/aubergine/eggplant
	Kancha kanthal	Green jackfruit
	Gajar	Carrot
	Turai	Ridged gourd
	Kacha kela	Green banana/plantain

	HINDI	ENGLISH
VEGETABLES (cont.)	Ghuiyan	Taro/arum root
	Karela	Bitter gourd, bitter melon
	Kaddu	Pumpkin
	Lauki	Bottle gourd, calabash
	Hara Matar	Green peas
	Kele-ka-phool	Banana blossom
	Mooli	Daikon/white radish
	Neem patti	Margosa leaves
	Suran	Elephant yam
	Paan	Betel leaf
	Palak	Spinach
	Gobi	Cauliflower
	Pyaz	Onion
	Pyaz patti	Scallions
	Parval/palwal	Pointed gourd
	Shakarkhand	Sweet potato
	Saag	Spinach
	Salgam	Turnip
	Kheera	Cucumber
	Seem/papdi	Broad bean
	Sarson-ka-saag	Mustard greens
	Kele-ki-tana	White pith of banana plant stem
FRUITS & NUTS	Aam	Mango
	Ananas	Pineapple
	Caju	Cashew
	Mungphalli	Peanut
	Phool Makhana	Lotus seed
	Kela	Banana
	Santra	Orange
	Keri/kacha aam	Unripe green mango
	Kanthal	Jackfruit
	Kismis	Raisin
	Ber	Indian plum

	HINDI	ENGLISH
FRUITS & NUTS (cont)	Nimbu	Lemon
	Nariyal	Coconut
	Papita	Papaya
	Pista	Pistachio
	Amrood	Guava
	Imli	Tamarind
BREADS	Kachori	Fried wheat pastry with seasoned filling
	Luchi/poori	Puffed fried flour bread
	Paratha	Thick crispy bread griddle fried in ghee
	Pau roti	Loaf of leavened bread
	Chapatti	Unleavened whole wheat flour bread
SPICES AND SEASONING	Adrak	Ginger
	Bada elaichi	Black cardamom
	Dalchini	Cinnamon
	Dhania	Coriander seeds
	Dhania patta	Cilantro/coriander leaves
	Elaichi	Green cardamom
	Garam Masala	A spice mixture of cinnamon, cardamom and cloves.
	Kala Mirch	Black pepper
	Haldi	Turmeric
	Hing	Asafoetida
	Zaffran	Saffron
	Jaiphal	Nutmeg
	Javitri	Mace
	Jeera	Cumin
	Ajwain	Carom seeds
	Kalonji	Black cumin, black onion seed
	Hara Mirch	Green chilli
	Kari patta	Curry leaves
	Lavang	Cloves
	Saunf	Fennel
	Methi dana	Fenugreek seeds

	HINDI	ENGLISH
SPICES AND SEASONING (cont.)	Namak	Salt
	Khuskhus	Poppy seeds
	Pudina patti	Mint leaves
	Lasoon	Garlic
	Rai/Sarson	Mustard seeds
	Shahijeera	Aniseed
	Sukha lal mirch	Red dried chilli
	Tej patta	Bay leaf
	Til	Sesame seed

Oils

Herbal Massaging Oils

Nothing beats a great massage and having a great massage oil to match tends to add an extra zing.

A massage can be therapeutic or sensual, but after a yoga session, or tilling the fields, or doing the laundry, you'll probably pass on the sensual and get right to the more mundane administration of rejuvenating oil.

Massaging oils can be made at home and even customized to assist in a range of therapeutic rehabilitations.

Mustard and sesame oils are good for invigorating uses, coconut oil for cooling down the body, chillies and pepper for pain relief, and cardamom and cinnamon for stress.

Pain Relieving Massage Oil

This oil has a strong sulphurous odor which is a polite way of saying that it has a really unpleasant smell. Once administered, one is to be wrapped up completely and stay that way for an hour or more before taking a warm shower. This oil can stain clothing so skip wearing your fancy best.

Holy basil (tulsi) and margosa leaves are available at many Indian and Asian stores. Ask for them by their Indian names.

Mustard oil	200 ml/ 1 cup
Holy basil leaves/ Tulsi patta	40 g/ 2 tbsp heaped
Margosa leaves/ Neem Patta	40 g/ 2 tbsp heaped
Star anise	5
Cinnamon sticks -	2
Garlic pods	20 g/ 1 tbsp heaped
Dried red chillies	20 g/ 1 tbsp heaped

In a heavy-bottomed uncovered pot, simmer all ingredients for an hour. Stir occasionally. Remove the chillies if they show signs of burning and continue to simmer for another half hour. Strain the oil and discard all but the oil. Allow it to cool and bottle into sterilized glass jars. This will keep for at about two months without signs of rancidity or staleness.

It should be administered slightly warm to the body in slow, powerful strokes and kneaded into the muscles.

Stress Relieving Oil

This oil is useful for stress relieving head massages or it can be applied to the joints.

Coconut oil	200 ml/ 1 cup
Fenugreek seeds	a pinch
Cinnamon sticks	6
Cardamom	15 pods
Fennel seeds	10 g/ 2 tsp
Cloves	5 buds
Fresh fragrant roses, stalks removed	4

In a heavy-bottomed uncovered pot, simmer all ingredients for an hour. Strain the oil and discard all but the oil. Allow it to cools and bottle into sterilized glass jars. Store in a cool place and it will keep for about two months.

In the event the oil should turn solid due to cold weather, just warm it up a bit before using it.

Floral Oil

This oil can be prepared with any combination of fragrant flowers. The blossoms may be old and dried up or even petals alone, although any damp ones on which fungus has begun to grow should not be used. Marigolds add color that may stain clothing. Lavender is considered a stress reliever. Rose is thought to improve blood circulation. Olive oil can be used instead of coconut oil.

Coconut oil	200 ml/ 1 cup
Marigold flowers	150 g/ 3/4 cup
Lavender	50 g/ 1/4 cup
Roses	100 g/ 1/2 cup
Vanilla beans	2
Cardamom	5 pods

Heat the oil until it smokes. Lower the flame and add the rest of the ingredients. Simmer for half an hour. Remove from heat and leave it uncovered in a cool place for an hour. Strain and reserve the oil in sterilized glass jars, and discarding the rest of the ingredients.

Store this oil in a cool place and it will keep for about a month.

Orange and Cardamom Balm

This is a somewhat contemporary recipe and used mainly in modern spas. It is quite refreshing.

Beeswax can be bought at many high-end beauty stores or can be purchased online.

Oranges	6
Cardamom	15 pods
Cinnamon sticks	2
Beeswax pearls	100 g/ 1/2 cup
Petroleum jelly	100 g/ 1/2 cup

Peel the oranges and remove the white pith from the skin. Chop the skin fine and add it to a heavy-bottomed pan with the other ingredients. Simmer the mixture on low heat for an hour, stirring occasionally. Strain and reserve the liquid in a sterilized container, discarding the residual. It will solidify when it cools.

About the Food Recipes

India has had a rich and varied history of which a major part lies in obscurity because it was not written down. In ancient days things were passed on to the next generation orally. Documenting these recipes has helped me to rediscover my country, my heritage, and the great spiritual heritage this land has bequeathed me. I have travelled extensively, following the paths that once were travelled by extraordinary people who performed extraordinary deeds. People have cooked for me and, in turn, I have cooked for them with the purpose of rekindling diet that has survived through the ages--diet so powerful that the ancients documented recipes that strengthen the body, expand the mind, and free the consciousness. This is a far cry from our present fast-food generation's doctrine—heighten the cholesterol, expand the waist, and open the wallet.

The ancient yogis believed that a lacto-vegetarian diet was the most beneficial one for the human body. They consumed milk and dairy products as supplements to their vegetarian fare. The followers of veganism at about that same time generally followed the same recipes but substituted the ghee with oil and eliminated paneer, the traditional home-made cheese.

What every yogi looked for in their diet was that the food be satvic (pure). Sometimes their colleagues might bend the rules a bit by adding onions or garlic to obtain its medicinal properties, but they generally stuck to a pure satvic diet.

Most of the recipes in this book are satvic. When I have encountered a recipe that uses onion or garlic, I have not altered it to suit the book, but have copied it faithfully.

As stated earlier, most of the recipes are for four people. For those not familiar with the "regular" Indian meal, this yield may be too little. Indians usually have two or more dishes at a meal attended by a lentil preparation and rice or bread. If you are preparing a one-dish meal you may have to double the recipe.

If you wish to correspond with me or would like to follow my regular blog, you can do that at chefzubin.com

Happy reading and happier cooking!!

Drinks Anyone?

The life of a yogi involves a great amount of physical activity apart from the daily chores are an integral part of the monastic/hermitage way of life. In addition to that, the heat and humidity of India's regular weather patterns boils off fluids requiring a large fluid intake. It is no mystery that the guys who do several hours of headstands in a day will also be the ones who have arrived at some tasty innovative solutions.

Yogurt and Mint Leaf Cooler

Yogurt	400g/ 2 cups/ 2 cups
Cumin seeds	a pinch
Peppercorns	a pinch
Chopped fresh ginger	10 g/ 2 tsp
Chopped fresh chillies	5 g/ 1 tsp
Chopped mint leaves	5 g/ 1 tsp
Salt	5 g/ 1 tsp

In a hot, dry pan, toast the cumin and the peppercorns separately until they change color. Crush them to a coarse powder with a mortar and pestle.

Whisk the yogurt in a bowl with 200 ml/1 cup of water and the rest of the ingredients. Taste and adjust the seasonings if required. Refrigerate and serve chilled.

Coconut and Kokum Drink

Sol Kadi

The kokum berry, which is often known in English as wild mangosteen is an evergreen native to the areas on the western coast of India. (See: http://en.wikipedia.org/wiki/Garcinia_indica)

The fruit is sun-dried prior to sale. The fresh fruits are rarely used for cooking.

The use of this fruit is often confined to the areas in which they grow. It imparts a characteristic sour taste and has had a long history associated with Indian cooking and ayurveda. It is widely believed that the juice of the berry relieves a variety of stomach ailments and is often used as a digestive.

The dried fruit is available at most Asian and Indian food stores.

Sol kadi is often served with rice.

Dried kokum berries	10
Grated coconut	200 g/ 1 cup packed tight
Green chillies	4
Chopped garlic	a pinch
Salt	to taste

Grind the coconut with the chillies, garlic, and about 50 ml/¼ cup of water in a food processor, squeeze out and save the thick milk, discarding the rest.

Soak the kokum in warm water and set aside for half an hour. Squeeze out and reserve the liquid by mashing through a strainer, discarding the pulpy remains.

Mix the coconut milk, kokum water, and salt. Taste and adjust the seasoning if required. Serve chilled.

Sweetened Yogurt and Powdered Cardamom Drink

Lassi

Yogurt	400g/2 cups
Cardamom	5 pods
Sugar	75 g/3/8 cup
Rose water	10 ml/2 tsp

Grind the cardamom pods with half the sugar in a food processor to obtain a fine powder. Pass this through a sieve and discard what remains in the sieve.

Whisk the yogurt in a bowl with the cardamom powder, sugar, rose water, and 100 ml/ ½ cup of water. Taste and adjust the sweetness if required. Refrigerate and serve chilled.

Honey and Lemon Cooler
Nimbu Pani

Honey   150 g/3/4 cup
Juice of 4 lemons
Mint leaves   5 g/ 1 tsp

Simmer 700 ml/ 3 ½ cups of water with the honey. Stir until the honey is melted. Remove from heat and set aside to cool.

Add the lemon juice and sprinkle the mint leaves. Serve over ice or refrigerate until chilled.

Rose Petal Tea
Gulabi Chai

Rose petal tea? Rose petal tea?!...Yes, I heard you the first time and ignored you. Yes! Rose petal tea! You will find it to be an extremely fragrant and totally refreshing drink. I love mine splashed over ice cubes. And you don't even need fresh petals. That bunch from Valentine's day, withering and drying up in the vase in the corner will do just fine.

Rose petals	20 g/1 tbsp heaped
Fennel seeds	10 g/ 2 tsp
Green cardamom pods	2
Cinnamon stick	1
Honey	50 g/ ¼ cup
Lemon juice	5 ml/ 1 tsp
Shredded mint leaves	a pinch

Lightly roast the fennel seeds in a pan and bring them to a boil with rose petals, cardamom, cinnamon and about 500 ml/ 2 ½ cups of water. Reduce the heat and simmer until the liquid has reduced to half.

Pour the honey, mint, and lemon juice into glasses and strain the liquid into them. Stir until the honey dissolves and serve warm or chilled.

Spiced Tea
Garam Masala Chai

This spiced tea is quite different from the "masala chai" that most people have come to expect. This brew does not contain tea leaves and is thus not stimulating. Coupled with a warm oil massage one will be headed to complete relaxation.

This spiced tea is also prescribed for colds, congestion, and digestive problems.

Cardamom	10 pods
Cinnamon	2 sticks
Cloves	6 buds
Fennel seeds	a pinch
Cumin seeds	a pinch
Honey	50 g/ ¼ cup

Individually roast the cardamom, cinnamon, cloves, fennel and cumin until they begin to change color. Simmer them in 500 ml/ 2 ½ cups of water for twenty minutes. Remove from heat and strain the tea, discarding the spices. Stir in the honey until it melts and serve warm.

Papaya, Ginger, and Coconut Milk Cooler
Narkol Pepeyer Rosha

Papayas have featured prominently in yogic and ayurvedic diets. Referred to as a "wonder-fruit," it is often prescribed in ancient Indian texts.

Peeled ripe papaya	400g/ 2 cups
Coconut milk	500 ml/ 2 ½ cups
Peeled and chopped ginger	10 g/ 2 tsp
Palm sugar	50 g/ 1/4 cup
Crushed black pepper	a pinch
Chopped mint leaves	5 g/ 1 tsp

In a food processor, blend together the papaya, coconut milk, ginger, palm sugar and black pepper to get a smooth juice. Stir in the chopped mint and serve chilled.

Beetroot, Orange, and Ginger Juice

Beetroots are often used in detoxifying diets. They are flavorful, have high fiber content.

Beetroot	400g/ 2 cups/ 2 cups
Orange juice	500 ml/ 2 ½ cups
Peeled ginger	10 g/ 2 tsp
Salt	a pinch
Crushed black pepper	a pinch
Lime juice	50 ml/ ¼ cup
Brown sugar (optional)	50 g/ 1/4 cup

Wash the beetroot well and boil them for twenty minutes until they are soft. Peel and puree them. Add the orange juice, ginger, salt, pepper, lime juice, and sugar. Blend well until you get a smooth juice. Serve chilled or at room temperature.

Carrot, Apple, and Ginger Juice

This drink is a great source of dietary fiber. It is drunk in detox therapies and frequently during days when fasting is observed.

Apples	450 g/1 lb
Carrots	200 g/1 cup
Ginger	10 g/2 tsp
Crushed black pepper	5 g/1 tsp
Chopped mint leaves	5 g/1 tsp
Lemon juice	20 ml/1 tbsp

Wash the apples thoroughly, but do not peel them. Prepare as rough dice. Peel, wash, and rough-chop the carrots and the ginger. Place the apples, carrots, ginger, black pepper and 200 ml/1 cup of distilled water into a blender and blend until smooth. Place in a bowl and whisk in the mint leaves and lemon juice. Serve chilled.

Appetizers and Soups

Indian meals are traditionally served with all of the dishes in the meal being placed before the diner simultaneously. The diner may pick and choose the combinations or alter the sequence to their liking.

It was only until I was well into my culinary education that the theory of courses as laid down by the French culinary greats began to sink in for me. My first attempts at educating my family ended in frustration when they declared that they understood the principle and served me curries chopped into fine bits followed by succulent kebabs.

My family...and the rest of this country have come a long way. Globalization has enabled us to understand the gastronomic difference of friends from all over the globe. So, when they are invited to dine at our house, we empathize with their dietary requirements, understand the manner in which they would like to be served, ignore them, and serve all the food simultaneously anyway! This is because the best way to eat Indian food is to play with flavors and textures, combining them all, and generally to be certain that you get your finger into every possible curried pie!

Spiced Okra and Pomello Salad

Bhindichya Katta

Okra	400g/ 2 cups
Mustard oil	20 ml
Turmeric powder	5 g/ 1 tsp
Chopped ginger	20 g/ 1 heaping tbsp
Chopped fresh chillies	10 g/ 2 tsp
Chopped raw mangoes	20 g/ 1 heaping tbsp
Chopped tomatoes	40 g/ 2 heaping tbsp
Salt	to taste
Chopped coriander leaves	10 g/ 2 tsp
Deseeded pomello or grapefruit flesh	200 g/ 1 cup

Pomello is available at Indian groceries at certain times of the year. Check with your purveyor. Trim the okra at either end and make a slit on one side from the top to the bottom. Heat the oil in a pan until it smokes, and add the okra. When it begins to turn bright green, add the turmeric, ginger, chillies, mangoes, and tomatoes. Stir for a few minutes until the tomatoes become pulpy. Stir in the salt and half of the coriander leaves and remove from the heat.

Allow the okra to cool and then mix it with the pomello and the remaining coriander leaves. Taste and adjust the seasonings if required and serve chilled.

Citrus Salad with Crumbled Paneer

Narangi Salad

Unlike most forms of fasting, religion-ordered fasts in India tend to be different. While most religions propagate fasts that are a form of corporal mortification, in India it is a disguised form of detoxification.

Over the centuries, the various gods in the Indian pantheon have largely been placed as bogeymen. Entreaties toward preserving health and safety were largely ignored unless it was a requirement as part of a larger ceremony to pay obeisance or appeasement to one or more of the gods. Since the climate in this country is not suited to gluttons (except lead-lined stomach-owners like me) a series of fasts and detoxifications was devised. During such an Indian religious fast, one can eat fruits, milk products, and sweets. Under *those* parameters, I could fast every day!

During one of those fasts, I was served this salad that really made me marvel at the creativity and contrast of flavors and colors, all packaged deliciously.

Pomello segments	200 g/ 1 cup
Orange segments	150 g/ 3/4 cup
Crumbled paneer	100 g/ 1/2 cup
Oil	20 ml/ 1 tbsp
Cumin seeds	a pinch
Fennel seeds	a pinch
Chopped fresh chillies	10 g/ 2 tsp
Lemon juice	10 ml/ 2 tsp
Chopped ginger	10 g/ 2 tsp
Crushed black peppercorns	5 g/ 1 tsp

Salt	to taste
Mint leaves	10 g/ 2 tsp

Place the pomello and orange segments in a bowl with a pinch of salt. Heat the oil and add the cumin and fennel until they splutter, add the green chillies, simmer for twenty seconds and pour the entire mixture over the citrus fruits. Add the lemon juice, ginger, peppercorns, salt and mint leaves. Taste and adjust the seasonings if required, sprinkle on the crumbled paneer (see page 86) and serve chilled.

Sprouted Bean Salad with Mint Leaves
Ankurit Moong ka Bhel

Bean sprouts	200 g/ 1 cup
Chopped tomatoes	100 g/ 1/2 cup
Shredded ginger	10 g/ 2 tsp
Red chilli powder	5 g/ 1 tsp
Lemon juice	20 ml/ 1 tbsp
Crushed black peppercorns	5 g/ 1 tsp
Mint leaves	10 g/ 2 tsp
Chopped coriander leaves	5 g/ 1 tsp
Sugar	a pinch
Salt	to taste

Mix together all the ingredients in a bowl. Taste, and adjust the seasonings. Serve chilled.

Watermelon and Ginger Salad
Adraki Tarbouj ka Salad

Diced watermelon	200 g/ 1 cup
Chopped ginger	20 g/ 1 heaping tbsp
Cracked black pepper	10 g/ 2 tsp
Mint leaves	10 g/ 2 tsp

| Lemon juice | 20 ml/ 1 tbsp |
| Salt | to taste |

Mix together all the ingredients and serve chilled

Roasted Pumpkin Salad with Mustard and Honey

Sarson Kadoo

Pumpkin, peeled and sliced thin	200 g/ 1 cup
Salt-	to taste
Mustard seeds	20 g/ 1 heaping tbsp
Peeled garlic	20 g/ 1 heaping tbsp
Honey	20 ml/ 1 tbsp
Cracked black peppercorns	5 g/ 1 tsp
Oil	20 ml/ 1 tbsp
Roasted coriander seeds -	5 g/ 1 tsp
Chopped coriander -	5 g/ 1 tsp

Soak the mustard seeds in a bowl of warm water for about twenty minutes and then grind them to a coarse paste in a food processor.

Pound the garlic and roasted coriander seeds together with a mortar and pestle. Add to a bowl and gently whisk in the black peppercorns, mustard paste and oil. Marinate for 10-15 minutes. Roast in a pre-heated oven at 300*F/ 160*C for about twelve minutes until they are soft.

Whisk the honey, chopped coriander, and a bit of salt, if required, with the remainder of the marinade and add with the roasted pumpkin. Serve warm.

Carrot and Roasted Almond Salad

Gajar Badaam ka Salad

| Grated carrots | 200 g/ 1 cup |
| Sliced almonds | 20 g/ 1 heaping tbsp |

Date or palm sugar or demerara	a pinch
Oil	10 ml/ 2 tsp
Lemon juice	20 ml/ 1 tbsp
Roasted coriander seeds	a pinch
Shredded spinach leaves	50 g/ ¼ cup packed tight
Shredded ginger	10 g/ 2 tsp
Shredded cucumber	50 g/ ¼ cup packed tight
Grated white radish	40 g/ 2 heaping tbsp
Cracked peppercorns	10 g/ 2 tsp
Salt	to taste
Mint leaves	5 g/ 1 tsp
Chopped coriander leaves	5 g/ 1 tsp

Toast the almonds in a dry pan until they are golden and set aside. Whisk together the sugar, oil, lemon juice, coriander seeds, and salt until the sugar dissolves completely. Mix together the carrot, spinach leaves, ginger, cucumber, radish, black peppercorns, mint leaves, and coriander leaves. Add the dressing and add until all the vegetables are coated. Taste and adjust the seasoning if necessary. Serve chilled.

Roasted Pineapple Salad

Ananas ka Salad

Rameshji, until his death a year ago, was my guru for a major part of my life. I really disliked our early encounters. I was on a mission (or so I thought), brimming with passion, youth, impatience, and the hot blood that flows within the veins of so many like me. He, on the other hand, was a placid, tranquil, extremely gifted yogi who had a way of answering my questions with a touch of deep-rooted philosophy that required a great deal of soul-searching of me. Each answer I received seemed to me like a set of clues that would stoke the fires of enthusiasm in Sherlock Holmes. Rameshji was extremely fond of pineapple, and knowing that it is considered by ayurveda as an aphrodisiac, he reserved them as a special treat. On a day when my chores were not so heavy, I prepared a salad that he gorged on. I guess this may have done the trick because, from then on, he answered my questions with an absolute and startling truth. I think I preferred when he answered with those many layers of philosophy.

Peeled, cored, and sliced pineapple	250 g/ 1 1/4 cup
Coriander seeds	a pinch
Fennel seeds	5 g/ 1 tsp
Black peppercorns	5 g/ 1 tsp
Chopped ginger	5 g/ 1 tsp
Chopped fresh chillies	10 g/ 2 tsp
Oil	20 ml/ 1 tbsp
Salt	to taste
Mint leaves	10 g/ 2 tsp

Rub a bit of oil into the pineapple slices and roast in a pre-heated oven or toast them in a non-stick pan until they turn golden.

Individually roast the coriander seeds, fennel seeds, and black peppercorns in a dry pan until they change color. Pound them coarsely with a mortar and pestle or grind in a food processor. Add to the pineapple along with the ginger, fresh chillies, salt, mint leaves, and any oil that remains. Taste and adjust the seasonings if required. Serve warm.

Beetroot and Toasted Sesame Seed Salad

Chukandar aur Til ka Salad

Beetroot	300 g/ 1 ½ cup
Sesame seeds	40 g/ 2 heaping tbsp
Mustard seeds	10 g/ 2 tsp
Fresh chillies	10 g/ 2 tsp
Chopped ginger	20 g/ 1 heaping tbsp
Lemon juice	10 ml/ 2 tsp
Chopped tomatoes	50 g/ 1/4 cup
Salt	to taste
Chopped coriander leaves	5 g/ 1 tsp

Boil the beetroot until they are soft, peel, slice, and set aside.

Toast the sesame seeds in a hot, dry pan until they are golden. Remove from heat and set aside.

Soak the mustard seeds in warm water for tewnty minutes and then grind them coarsely along with the fresh chillies in a food processor. To this blend, add 50g/ 2 oz of the beetroot with the ginger, lemon juice, and salt.

Add this blend to the sliced beetroots along with the chopped tomatoes and more salt if necessary. Taste and adjust the seasoning if necessary. Sprinkle on the sesame seeds and coriander leaves and serve.

Yogurt and Spiced Rice

Thair Sadam

This is a wonderful dish. It is great as an appetizer, salad, or main course. It is light and filling and can sooth an upset digestive system.

Raw rice	200 g/ 1 cup
Green mango, peeled and chopped	50 g/ 1/4 cup
Cucumber, peeled, seeds removed and chopped	50 g/ 1/4 cup
Chopped fresh chillies	5 g/ 1 tsp
Chopped coriander leaves	10 g/ 2 tsp
Yogurt	500 g/ 2 ½ cups
Shredded ginger	5 g/ 1 tsp
Salt	to taste
Milk	150 ml/ ¾ cup
Oil	40 ml/ 2 tbsp
Mustard seeds	a pinch
Dried red chillies	5
Curry leaves	1 sprig

Rinse the rice until rinse water runs clear. Boil the rice in water with salt until it is quite soft. Mash the rice and set aside.

In a bowl, mix together the rice, chopped mango, cucumber, fresh chillies, ginger, coriander leaves, yogurt, salt, and milk.

In a pan, heat the oil. Toss in the mustard seeds, dried red chillies and the curry leaves. When the seeds crackle, pour the entire oil-spice mixture over the rice. Stir the rice and evenly mix in the spices and seasonings. Taste and adjust the seasonings if required. Serve chilled.

Spiced Banana Kebabs

Keley ke Tikkiyan

Green (raw) bananas (plantains) are available at most Asian and Caribbean stores. They are quite healthy, easy to work with, and exude a wonderful earthy texture and fragrance.

Green bananas	300 g/ 1 ½ cup
Oil	20 ml/ 1 tbsp
Cumin seeds	a pinch
Coriander seeds	a pinch
Chopped ginger	10 g/ 2 tsp
Chopped fresh chillies	10 g/ 2 tsp
Salt	to taste
Fresh coriander leaves	10 g/ 2 tsp
Semolina	50 g/ 1/4 cup
Ghee	20 g/ 1 tbsp
Juice of one lemon	

Peel and chop the green bananas and set aside. Heat the oil and add the cumin and coriander seeds, stirring until they turn golden. Add the banana, ginger, fresh chillies, and salt and stir for a few minutes until the bananas are soft and have a pasty texture. Stir in the coriander leaves, taste and adjust the seasoning, if required. Divide the dough into eight even-sized balls, roll them in the semolina and flatten them in the palm of your hands. Heat the ghee in a non-stick pan, fry the banana cutlets on either side until they are evenly golden and crisp. Serve hot with chutneys.

Pan-seared Taro Patties

Zimmikhand ke tikkiyan

Grated taro	200 g/ 1 cup
Oil	20 ml/ 1 tbsp

Cumin seeds	5 g/ 1 tsp
Chopped ginger	10 g/ 2 tsp
Chopped green chillies –	5 g/ 1 tsp
Salt	to taste
Chopped coriander leaves –	5 g/ 1 tsp

Heat the oil in a heavy-bottomed pot and add in the cumin seeds. When they crackle, add the taro, ginger, and green chillies. Cook until the taro softens, stir in a bit of salt and mash it to a thick paste. Knead in the coriander leaves and form the mixture into small patties. Grill or fry with a bit of oil in a non-stick pan until they are golden and crisp on the outside. Serve hot with chutneys.

Steamed Colocassia (Taro) Leaves
Paatra

Colocassia (Taro) is a tuber that is similar in taste and texture to yam. In fact there are several similar preparations that use yam leaves instead. These tubers are grown rather easily and almost every hermitage garden has a tiny patch dedicated to them. Taro leaves can be found in some Asian markets, especially Filipino markets.

This is a healthy snack readily available all over Gujarat and Maharashtra.

Colocassia/arvi leaves	6 leaves
Gram flour	200 g/ 1 cup
Whole-wheat flour	20 g/ 1 tbsp
Yogurt	20 g/ 1 tbsp
Turmeric powder	a pinch
Fresh chillies ground to a paste	a pinch
Ginger paste	a pinch
Palm or Demerara sugar –	5 g/ 1 tsp
Oil	20 ml/ 1 tbsp
Mustard seeds	a pinch
Cumin seeds	a pinch
Salt	to taste
Chopped coriander leaves	5 g/ 1 tsp
Juice of one lemon	

Wash the colocassia leaves and cut them into halves. Pat dry and set aside.

In a bowl, mix together the gram flour, wheat flour, yogurt, turmeric, fresh chilli paste, ginger paste, sugar, half of the oil, and enough water to make a thick smooth paste.

Lay the leaves out flat on a work surface and spread a bit of the gram flour-spice mixture evenly over each. Roll it from one end to the other to get a tight cylinder. Steam it covered for 15 minutes and remove when cooked through.

Set aside to cool and then slice the rolls into thick even disks.

In a pan heat the remaining oil and add the mustard and cumin seeds. When the seeds crackle, pour over the patra slices. Drizzle on the lemon juice and serve garnished with coriander leaves.

Spinach and Pine Nut Kebabs

Hara Tikki

Spinach leaves, rinsed clean,	900 g/ 2 lbs
Potatoes	300 g/ 1 ½ cups
Pine nuts	40 g/ 2 heaping tbsp
Bengal gram flour/ Besan	50 g/ ¼ cup
Chopped fresh chillies	10 g/ 2 tsp
Turmeric powder	5 g/ 1 tsp
Crushed black peppercorns	5 g/ 1 tsp
Chopped ginger	10 g/ 2 tsp
Salt	to taste
Chopped coriander leaves	5 g/ 1 tsp
Ghee	40 g/ 2 heaping tbsp

Drop the spinach leaves into boiling, salted water. Remove them when they turn bright green and plunge them into ice-cold water to stop the cooking process. Rough-chop the spinach leaves and squeeze them in a kitchen towel to drain off the excess liquid.

Peel, cut and boil the potatoes until they are soft. Mash them and set aside.

Toast the pine nuts in a dry pan until they change color. Crush them coarsely with a mortar and pestle.

In a bowl, mix together the spinach, potatoes, pine nuts, gram flour, chillies, turmeric, peppercorns, ginger, coriander leaves and salt. Knead them until the mixture feels firm. Divide them into evenly round, lemon-sized balls and keep aside

Heat a bit of the ghee in a non-stick pan, flatten the balls with your palms to form thick discs and shallow-fry until they are evenly golden and crisp on the outside and cooked through. Serve hot with chutneys.

Lentil and Dried Fruit Fritters

Mannuka Vada

Every once in a while an extravagant donation of dried fruits and nuts might find its way into the ashram. This can be turned into an absolutely amazing repast.

Split Bengal gram/ Chana Dal	150 g/ 3/4 cup
Split black lentils	150 g/ 3/4 cup
Chopped fresh chillies	10 g/ 2 tsp
Chopped coriander leaves	10 g/ 2 tsp
Chopped mint leaves	5 g/ 1 tsp
Chopped ginger	10 g/ 2 tsp
Salt	to taste
Raisins	40 g/ 2 heaping tbsp
Cashew nuts	20 g/ 1 heaping tbsp
Oil	to deep fry
Juice of one lemon	

Wash the lentils and soak them separately in water for three hours until they soften. Drain off the excess water.

Remove a third of the split Bengal gram and set aside. Grind the rest of the lentils to a coarse paste in a food processor. Mix together the ground lentils, the soaked Bengal gram, chillies, coriander, mint, ginger, salt, raisins, and cashew nuts.

Heat the oil in a pan and spoon the mixture in a bit at a time. Fry at moderate heat and turn over the lentil dollops until they are evenly golden and crisp.

Remove from the oil with a slotted spoon and drain on an absorbent kitchen paper towel. Sprinkle on the lemon juice and serve hot with chutneys.

Green Pea Soup with Burnt Garlic

Lassoni Muttar ka Shorba

Green peas	300 g/ 1 ½ cups
Oil	20 ml/ 1 tbsp
Cumin seeds	a pinch
Asafoetida	a pinch
Chopped ginger	5 g/ 1 tsp
Salt	to taste
Crushed black peppercorns	5 g/ 1 tsp
Ghee	10 g/ 2 tsp
Chopped garlic	10 g/ 2 tsp
Chopped mint leaves	a pinch
Chopped coriander leaves	a pinch
Juice of one lemon	

Heat the oil in a heavy-bottomed pot and add the cumin seeds and asafoetida and roast until they change color. Add the green peas, ginger, salt, and black peppercorns. Simmer for a couple of minutes. Pour in 600 ml/ 3 cups of water and simmer for ten minutes until the peas are soft. Crush the peas coarsely in a food processor, taste and adjust the seasoning and thickness, if required. Set aside.

Heat the ghee in a pan and stir in the garlic on low heat until it turns a deep golden. Pour the mixture into the ground pea base. Stir in the chopped mint, coriander and lemon juice. Serve hot.

Curried Papaya Soup with Coconut Milk

Pepey Sorr

I love papaya. The first time I treated papaya in this manner I was apprehensive because I could not imagine wanting to cook a beautifully ripened papaya. I was pleasantly surprised by the flavor and ultimately mystified as to the kind of genius who had come up with this brilliant idea in the first place.

Papayas are often eaten to clear out the stomach and digestive tracts. I have used it extensively as part of a detox therapy and diet.

Peeled and diced papaya	400g/ 2 cups
Ghee	10 g/ 2 tsp
Fennel seeds	a pinch
Cinnamon stick	1
Chopped ginger	20 g/ 1 heaping tbsp
Chopped fresh chillies	20 g/ 1 heaping tbsp
Turmeric powder	10 g/ 2 tsp
Coconut milk	500 ml/ 2 ½ cups
Salt	to taste
Grated nutmeg	5 g/ 1 tsp
Chopped mint leaves	5 g/ 1 tsp
Juice of one lemon	optional

Heat the ghee in a pot and add in the fennel and cinnamon. When the seeds begin to change color, add the papaya, ginger, chillies, and turmeric. Stir on low heat for a minute or so to get rid of the raw spice flavor. Add in 200 ml/ 1 cup of water and simmer for ten minutes until the papaya is soft. Add the coconut milk and salt and simmer for another twenty minutes until the coconut milk begins to thicken. Mash some of the papaya roughly with a spoon and increase the heat. Boil the soup rapidly for half a minute, taste and adjust the seasonings if necessary. Remove from heat and stir in the mint and lemon. Serve hot.

Yogurt and Gram Flour Curry
Kadhi

Kadhi is a generic name for this yogurt-based gravy. It is consumed in large quantities in the regions of Rajasthan, Kutch, and Marwar. It is quite cooling and can be made thin to be served as a soup or thickened to become a gravy.

It is rather easy to prepare and served often as part of a light lunch.

Yogurt -	500 g/ 2 ½ cups
Gram flour/ Besan	100 g/ ½ cup
Turmeric Powder	10 g/ 2 tsp
Cardamom Pods	5
Oil	40 ml/ 2 tbsp

Sliced Onions	150 g/ 3/4 cup
Mustard seeds	a pinch
Fenugreek seeds / Methi Dana	a pinch
Powdered Asafoetida/Hing	a pinch
Dried Red Chillies	5
Fresh chillies cut in half	3
Chopped coriander leaves	5 g/ 1 tsp
Salt	To taste

Whisk together the yogurt, gram flour, and turmeric until all lumps have disappeared.

In a pot, heat the oil and add the mustard seeds, fenugreek seeds, asafoetida, and green cardamom pods. Stir until the seeds crackle. Break the red chillies in half and add them in. Add in the sliced onions and cook until the onions are soft and translucent. Add in the yogurt-gram flour mix and bring it to a boil.

Add in the fresh chillies and let it simmer for 10 minutes. Taste and adjust the seasoning. Simmer for another 10 minutes until the gravy thickens sufficiently to coat the back of a spoon. Finish with green coriander leaves and serve hot with plain boiled rice.

Pumpkin and Ginger Soup with Fennel
Adraki Kadoo ka Shorba

Pumpkin, peeled and cut into cubes	500 g/ 2 ½ cups
Ghee	10 g/ 2 tsp
Fennel seeds	5 g/ 1 tsp
Curry leaves	a sprig
Coriander seeds	a pinch
Chopped fresh chillies	10 g/ 2 tsp
Chopped ginger	40 g/ 2 heaping tbsp
Turmeric powder	10 g/ 2 tsp
Salt	to taste
Chopped coriander leaves	10 g/ 2 tsp
Juice of one lemon	

Heat the ghee in a heavy-bottomed pot and add in the fennel, curry leaves, and coriander seeds. When the seeds crackle, add the pumpkin, chillies, ginger, turmeric powder, and salt. Stir on low heat for ten minutes until the pumpkin begins to soften. Pour a litre/ 5 cups of water over the mixture and simmer covered for twenty minutes until the pumpkin has softened completely. Smash the pumpkin roughly with a ladle and bring the liquid to a boil for a minute. Taste and adjust the seasonings, if required. Remove from the heat and stir in the lemon juice and coriander leaves. Serve hot.

Spiced Eggplant Soup with Mint
Baingan ka Shorba

What!? Eeggplant soup!? Well, those were my sentiments exactly when I first heard of this absolutely wonderful concoction. I could not imagine how justice could be done to a soup using eggplant as the main ingredient.

This recipe dates back more than 2,000 years to the time when the Indians traded with the Egyptians and Assyrians.

Eggplant	600 g/ 1 ½ lbs
Ghee	20 g/ 1 heaping tbsp
Carom seeds	a pinch
Black peppercorns	10
Cinnamon	1 stick
Cardamom	6 pods
Bay leaves	2
Chopped fresh chillies	10 g/ 2 tsp
Chopped ginger	20 g/ 1 heaping heaping tbsp
Salt	to taste
Chopped mint leaves	10 g/ 2 tsp
Juice of one lemon	

Roast the eggplants individually on an open heat until the skin turns dark and crisps. Peel off the skin, discard the seeds from the center and rough-chop the flesh.

Heat the ghee in a heavy-bottomed pot and add the carom seeds, peppercorns, cinnamon, cardamom, and bay leaves. When the spices begin to change color, add in the chopped eggplant flesh, chillies, ginger, and salt. Stir for a few minutes on medium heat and then pour 800 ml/ 4 cups of water over the mixture. Simmer the soup for half an hour to allow the flavors to develop. Bring it to a boil for a minute, taste, and adjust seasonings if required. Remove from heat and stir in the lemon juice and mint leaves. Serve hot with an optional drizzle of cream.

Spiced Mango Soup with Asafoetida
Aam ka Turus

A "Turus" is a fruity soup that is made in the summer to replace a meal. It is part of a detoxifying regimen and considered highly effective in flushing unwanted elements from the body.

Most pulpy fruits can be used to make a turus although mangoes are definitely my favorite.

Ripe mangoes	800 g/ 4 cups
Turmeric powder	5 g/ 1 tsp
Chopped fresh chillies	5 g/ 1 tsp
Salt	to taste
Ghee	20 g/ 1 heaping tbsp
Asafoetida	5 g/ 1 tsp
Mustard seeds	a pinch
Curry leaves	a sprig
Chopped mint leaves	10 g/ 2 tsp

Place the mangoes in a pre-heated oven (approximately 250C/475F) for fifteen minutes until the skin is roasted and the flesh soft. Peel. Reserve the flesh. Discard the skin and stone.

Place the flesh in a pot covered with 800ml/ 4 cups of water and simmer it with the turmeric, fresh chillies, and salt. Stir occasionally while simmering for fifteen minutes or more, until the soup begins to thicken. Bring to a boil for a minute and reduce the heat to a simmer again for twenty minutes to reduce the soup further.

Heat the ghee in a non-stick pan and add in the asafoetida, mustard seeds, and curry leaves. When the spices crackle, pour this mixture into the soup pot. Taste and adjust the seasoning. Remove from heat, strain, and discard the mango fibers, and sprinkle in the mint leaves. Serve hot.

Entrees

Bitter Gourd and Tamarind Curry

Kaipaikai Curry

Bitter gourd, also known as bitter melon or bitter pear, is a vegetable held in high esteem by yogis and lay persons alike. According to ayurvedic studies, the vegetable is said to have a variety of curative properties including the ability to purify and detoxify the blood, reduce diabetes, and soothe the digestive system.

The fact that the vegetable is bitter is all too apparent from its name, but there are ways to reduce the bitterness.

Rubbing the cleaned and cut vegetable with salt, leaving it in a cool place for half an hour, and then washing away the excess salt helps a lot. Some chefs fry the vegetable before cooking it add ing richness and a layer on the hips as well.

Bitter gourd	450 g/ 1 lb
Salt	to taste
Turmeric powder	20 g/ 1 heaping tbsp
Oil	20 ml/ 1 tbsp
Mustard seeds	a pinch
Chopped ginger	10 g/ 2 tsp
Coriander powder	5 g/ 1 tsp
Cumin powder	5 g/ 1 tsp
Palm or Demerara sugar	20 g/ 1 heaping tbsp
Tamarind pulp	50 g/ 1/4 cup
Chopped mint leaves	10 g/ 2 tsp

Roughly scrape the skin of the bitter gourd. In India, bitter gourds have a thin skin. Were you to peel it off there would be very litt flesh remaining. Plus, you do need the dietary fiber! Cut the gourd in half, discard the seeds, and cut it into inch-long pieces. Rub the pieces with salt and half the turmeric powder and set aside in a cool place for half an hour. Squeeze out the liquid and wash off the excess salt.

Heat the oil in a pan and add in the mustard seeds. When the seeds crackle, add the gourd pieces, remaining turmeric powder, ginger, coriander, cumin, sugar, and tamarind pulp. Add in 50 ml/ ¼ cup of water and simmer for a few minutes, stirring occasionally until the sugar melts. Bring the sauce to a boil, taste, and adjust the seasoning if required. Reduce the heat and simmer the sauce for two more minutes until the gourd is soft and cooked through. Stir in the mint leaves. Serve hot.

Bitter Gourd Stir-Fry

Karela Bhuni

Cleaned and sliced bitter gourd	450 g/ 1 lb
Sunflower oil	20 ml/ 1 tbsp
Cumin seeds/ jeera	5 g/ 1 tsp
Chopped onions	125 g/ 1 ¼ cup
Salt	to taste
Sugar	5 g/ 1 tsp
Chilli powder	5 g/ 1 tsp

In a heavy-bottomed pan, heat the oil and fry the sliced gourd until golden and crisp. Remove with a slotted spoon and drain on an absorbent kitchen paper towel.

Reheat the oil that remains in the pan, stir in the cumin seeds until they crackle. Reduce the heat and add in the onions and cook until they are brown and soft. Add in salt and chilli powder.

Add the fried gourd, stir well, and add the sugar. Toss a little and check seasoning. Serve hot.

Bitter Gourd Hash

Karela Bhate

A "bhate" is a traditional Bengali dish. The name signifies something that has been mashed. Bengalis use this as an accompaniment to the main meal and make several varieties using a combination of ingredients. You can make a pumpkin bhate using red pumpkin (the Halloween variety) or potato bhate, eggplant bhate, and even a beetroot bhate

Bitter gourd, cleaned	100 g/ ½ cup
Turmeric powder	a pinch
Boiled potato, peeled	150 g/ ¾ cup
Chopped fresh chillies	a pinch
Mustard oil	10 ml/ 2 tsp
Salt	to taste

Scrape the rough skin from the gourd and discard with the seeds. Cut into small pieces.

Boil in boiling, salted water to which the pinch of turmeric has been added. Remove and drain. mashing the gourd while it is still hot.

Add in the boiled potato, fresh chillies, mustard oil, and salt, continuing to mash to create a homogenous mixture.

Taste and adjust salt, if necessary. Serve at room temperature.

Spiced Braised Pumpkin

Hara Kaddu Masala

Tender young pumpkins are wonderful to prepare in this fashion. They are eaten all through summer as a means of cooling the body. They are said to prevent the onset of acid reflux and cramps.

Tender young pumpkins	600 g/ 3 cups
Oil	20 ml/ 1 tbsp
Mustard seeds	a pinch
Curry leaves	one sprig
Dried red chillies	2 pieces
Sliced onions	100 g/ ½ cup
Chopped green chillies	5 g/ 1 tsp
Shredded ginger	5 g/ 1 tsp
Roasted coriander seeds	a pinch
Grated coconut	20 g/ 1 heaping tbsp
Salt	to taste

Sugar	a pinch
Amchur powder	a pinch
Chopped coriander leaves	5 g/ 1 tsp

Grate the skin and flesh of the pumpkin, discarding the inner pith and seeds. Heat the oil in a pot and add the mustard seeds, curry leaves, and red chillies. When the seeds begin to splutter, add in the sliced onions and stir them on low heat until they are soft and transparent. Add in the grated pumpkin, green chillies, and ginger. Continue to stir for about five minutes until the pumpkin is soft. Crush the coriander seeds and sprinkle over the pumpkin along with the coconut, salt, sugar, amchur, and the coriander leaves. Taste and adjust the seasoning, if required. Stir for a few minutes until the liquid is absorbed and the pumpkin is tender. Serve hot.

Pumpkin Dumplings Simmered in a Tangy Nut Gravy

Kaddu ke Koftey

Red pumpkin, peeled and cut into cubes	400g/ 2 cups
Chickpea flour/ besan	50 g/ ¼ cup
Oil	20 ml/ 1 tbsp
Cinnamon sticks	2
Green cardamom pods	4
Cloves	6 buds
Chopped onions	150 g/ ¾ cup
Slit green chillies	10 g/ 2 tsp
Chopped garlic	10 g/ 2 tsp
Shredded ginger	10 g/ 2 tsp
Tamarind pulp	15 ml/ 1 tbsp
Crushed cashew nuts	40 g/ 2 heaping tbsp
Salt	to taste
Chopped coriander leaves	5 g/ 1 tsp

Boil the pumpkin with a bit of salt until it is soft. Remove from the liquid, mash it, and squeeze in a piece of cheesecloth to drain off the excess liquid. Gently roast the chickpea flour in a dry pan and mix with the mashed pumpkin. Knead to form a soft dough. Form this dough into lemon-sized balls and drop them in a pot of boiling salted water. When they rise to the surface and appear to be done, remove them with a slotted spoon and set aside to cool.

Heat the oil in a pot. Add in the cinnamon, cardamom, and cloves. When the spices begin to swell, add the chopped onions and simmer until they are golden. Add in the chillies, garlic, and ginger. Stir occasionally until the garlic changes color. Add in the tamarind pulp, a bit of salt, and about 200 ml/ 1 cup of water and reduce the heat to a simmer. Taste and adjust the seasoning of the liquid, if required. Add the dumplings to the pot along with the nuts. Simmer until the liquid has thickened and begins to coat the dumplings. Increase the heat and bring the liquid to a boil, finish off with the coriander leaves. Serve hot.

Loofah (or Zucchini) with Coconut
Toari Bhajji

Loofah, which is also known as ridge gourd, is available fresh all across Southeast Asia. It is available in most Indian and Asian groceries.

Loofah is favored because of its high water content and the roughage that it provides. Very little preparation has to be done to it and it cooks in minutes.

To prepare the vegetable, simply run a peeler on the rough ridges and pare them down before washing and cutting them to desired sizes.

This recipe can be made using zucchini Use significantly less as loofah contains a lot of water, the weight of which steams out.

Loofah	900 g/ 2 lbs
Oil	20 ml/ 1 tbsp
Mustard seeds	a pinch
Curry leaves	a sprig
Chopped onions	50 g/ ¼ cup
Chopped garlic	10 g/ 2 tsp
Shredded ginger	10 g/ 2 tsp
Chopped fresh chillies	10 g/ 2 tsp
Salt	to taste
Grated coconut or desiccated coconut	40 g/ 2 heaping tbsp
Chopped coriander leaves	10 g/ 2 tsp

Use a peeler on the ridges of the gourd and then cut it into half lengthwise and then large dice.

Heat the oil in a pan and add the mustard seeds and curry leaves. When the seeds crackle, add the onions and cook them until they are soft. Add the garlic and stir until it begins to change color. Add the gourd, ginger, chillies, and salt. Simmer until the vegetable turns bright green and is soft. Mix in the coconut and taste to adjust the seasonings, if necessary. Add the coriander leaves and remove from heat. Serve hot.

Grilled Eggplant with Spiced Potatoes and Yogurt Sauce

Bharwaan Baingan Kadhi

Eggplant	200 g/ 1 cup
Potatoes	450 g/ 1 lb
Oil	20 ml/ 1 tbsp
Cumin seeds	a pinch
Coriander seeds	a pinch
Chopped fresh chillies	10 g/ 2 tsp
Chopped ginger	10 g/ 2 tsp
Chopped coriander leaves	5 g/ 1 tsp
Salt	to taste

For the yogurt sauce

Ghee	20 g/ 1 heaping tbsp
Cumin seeds	a pinch
Mustard seeds	a pinch
Asafoetida	a pinch
Chopped ginger	10 g/ 2 tsp
Fresh chillies	10 g/ 2 tsp
Chickpea flour/ Besan	20 g/ 1 heaping tbsp
Yogurt	400g/ 2 cups
Turmeric powder	10 g/ 2 tsp
Salt	to taste
Chopped coriander leaves	10 g/ 2 tsp
Chopped mint leaves	g/ 1 tsp

Cut the eggplant into thin slices lengthwise. Sprinkle with salt and grill them on a hot griddle plate or put them in a preheated oven (225⁰C/425⁰F) for about ten minutes until they turn soft. Set aside to cool.

Boil peeled potatoes and mash them roughly. Heat the oil in a pan and add the cumin and coriander seeds until they change color. Add the mashed potatoes, ginger, chillies and salt, and simmer for a few minutes. Add the fresh coriander and remove from heat. When the potato mixture is cool, form a lime-sized lump and place it at one end of the sliced eggplant and roll from one end to the other enveloping the potato mixture within the eggplant. Secure the eggplant in place with a toothpick.

For the sauce, heat the ghee in a heavy-bottomed pot and stir in the cumin seeds, mustard seeds, and asafoetida until they begin to change color. Add the ginger, chillies, and chickpea flour and stir until the flour is golden. Gently whip the yogurt until it is smooth and add it to the pot along with turmeric powder and salt. Simmer until the sauce thickens and drop in the stuffed eggplant rolls. Bring the sauce to a boil and when the yogurt coats the eggplant dumplings, stir in the coriander and mint. Remove from heat, taste, and adjust the seasonings, if necessary. After removing the toothpicks, serve with plain boiled white rice.

Smoked Eggplant Hash

Baingan Bharta

Although there is nothing to substitute for the smoky flavor this dish gets when it is cooked on coal embers, gas stoves do a good job. Ideal for the winter when plump shiny eggplants are plentiful, this dish is warm and nourishing.

Large black eggplant	450 g/ 1 lb
Mustard oil	20 ml/ 1 tbsp
Chopped fresh chillies	20 g/ 1 heaping tbsp
Chopped onion	50 g/ 1/4 cup
Chopped garlic	10 g/ 2 tsp
Turmeric powder	5 g/ 1 tsp
Chilli powder	a pinch
Salt	to taste
Chopped tomatoes	50 g/ ¼ cup
Sugar	5 g/ 1 tsp

Mustard seeds	a pinch
Cumin seeds	a pinch
Ghee	5 g/ 1 tsp

On an open heat, char the skin of the eggplant. Keep rotating until the skin is evenly charred and quite black. Cool. With the help of a knife remove the skin and separate the flesh from the seeds. Chop fine.

In a pan, heat the mustard oil until it smokes, reduce heat, and add in the mustard and cumin seeds. Stir until they crackle. Add in the chopped onion and stir until they are golden, add the garlic and cook until soft.

Put in the chopped eggplant flesh, the chopped chillies, turmeric, chilli powder, salt, and a pinch of sugar. Stir the mixture until it bubbles. Add in the tomatoes and simmer for five or more minutes until they are soft and pulpy. Check and adjust the seasoning, if required. Spoon ghee on top. Serve hot.

Stir-Fried Spinach and Fenugreek Leaves

Ghota Hua Palak aur Methi ka Saag

Cleaned fenugreek leaves/ methi patta–	100 g/ 1/2 cup
Cleaned spinach	250 g/ 1 1/4 cup
Dry red chilli	1
Cashew nut paste	20 g/ 1 heaping tbsp
Ginger paste	5 g/ 1 tsp
Chopped garlic	10 g/ 2 tsp
Chopped onions	20 g/ 1 heaping tbsp
Chopped tomatoes	40 g/ 2 heaping tbsp
Chopped fresh chilli	1
Cumin seeds	a pinch
Turmeric powder	a pinch
Chilli powder	a pinch
Cream	10 ml/ 2 tsp
Garam masala powder	a pinch
Ghee	5 g/ 1 tsp

Chopped coriander leaves	5 g/ 1 tsp
Salt	to taste
Chaat masala	a pinch

In boiling, salted water, blanch the spinach and fenugreek leaves separately. Remove and run them under cool water, squeeze out the excess water. Rough-chop the leaves and set aside.

In a pot, heat oil and add the cumin seeds and the dried red chilli. When the seeds crackle, add in the chopped onions and cook until they are golden. Add in the garlic and ginger paste, stirring for a few minutes until the garlic changes color. Add in the spinach, fenugreek, fresh chilli, turmeric, chilli powder, salt, and cashew nut paste. Keep stirring to mix well. If the leaves begin to burn, sprinkle in a little water. After cooking for a few minutes, add in the cream and reduce the heat to a simmer. Add the tomatoes and simmer until they are pulpy. Check and adjust seasoning. Sprinkle on the ghee and chaat masala. Stir Serve hot.

Fenugreek-Flavored Garbanzo Bean-Flour Curry

Methi Pithla

Garbanzo bean flour/ Gram flour / Besan	200 g/ 1 cup
Cleaned, washed and chopped fenugreek leaves	200 g/ 1 cup
Chopped onion	50 g/ 1/4 cup
Chopped fresh chillies	2
Oil	40 ml/ 2 tbsp
Mustard seeds	a pinch
Cumin seeds	a pinch
Dried red chillies	2
Turmeric powder	a pinch
Chopped coriander leaves	5 g/ 1 tsp
Salt	to taste

Mix the flour in two cups of water and whisk to ensure that there are no lumps. Set this aside.

Heat the oil in a pan and add in the mustard seeds, cumin seeds, and dried red chillies. When the seeds crackle, add in the chopped onions and cook until the onions are golden.

Add in the fenugreek leaves, chopped fresh chillies, and a bit of salt. Cook over moderate heat for a few minutes, stirring all the time. Add in the turmeric powder and the flour mix.

Reduce the heat and simmer until the sauce thickens. Taste and adjust the seasoning, if required. Serve hot garnished with chopped coriander leaves.

Carrot and Coconut Stir-Fry

Carrot Poriyal

Peeled and diced carrots	450 g/ 1 lb
Coconut oil	20 ml/ 1 tbsp
Mustard seeds	a pinch
Curry leaves	a sprig
Dried red chillies, halved	2
Udad dal dhuli/ split black lentils	a pinch
Chana dal dhuli/ split Bengal gram	a pinch
Hing/ asafoetida	a pinch
Turmeric powder	a pinch
Salt	to taste
Sugar	a pinch
Grated fresh coconut	40 g/ 2 heaping tbsp
Chopped coriander leaves	5 g/ 1 tsp

Heat the oil in a pot and add in the mustard, curry leaves, and dried red chillies. When the seeds splutter, add in the lentils and asafoetida. Stir gently until they change color. Add in the carrots, turmeric powder, salt, sugar, and about 80 ml of water. Simmer, stirring occasionally, until most of the liquid has been absorbed and the carrots are tender. Sprinkle in the grated coconut and coriander leaves and stir so that they are evenly mixed. Taste and adjust seasoning, if required. Serve hot.

Note: If fresh coconut is not available, desiccated coconut can be used.

Slow Braised Pumpkin with Sesame Seeds

Tilwale Kaddu

Red pumpkin peeled and cut into cubes	450 g/ 1 lb
Roasted sesame seeds	50 g/ 1/4 cup
Mustard oil	20 ml/ 1 tbsp
Mustard seeds	5 g/ 1 tsp
Coriander seeds	a pinch
Dried red chillies	4
Turmeric powder	10 g/ 2 tsp
Sugar	5 g/ 1 tsp
Salt	to taste
Chopped coriander leaves	5 g/ 1 tsp

Heat the oil until it smokes. Cool it down a bit and add the mustard seeds, coriander seeds, and dried red chillies. When the seeds crackle, add in the pumpkin and stir over high heat for about five minutes. Reduce the heat, add in the salt and turmeric powder, cover, and simmer for about ten minutes until the pumpkin is almost cooked through. Gently toast the sesame seeds in a dry pan and add it along with the sugar to the pumpkin. Keep cooking until the pumpkin is tender. Taste and adjust the seasoning, if required. Stir in the coriander leaves. Serve hot.

Eggplant Cooked with Margosa Leaves

Neem Begun

Neem leaves have always held an importance in ayurveda and Indian culture for its medicinal qualities. They are available from most Indian stores. At first I thought that this was going to be quite an unhappy pairing, but since I am always open to new culinary ideas, I tried it out. The tender neem leaves provide a unique twist to the eggplant. The refreshing sensation of the leaves combined with the earthiness of the eggplant works beautifully.

Eggplant, diced	150 g/ 3/4 cup
Tender neem leaves/ Margosa	20 g/ 1 heaping tbsp

Mustard oil	40 ml/ 2 tbsp
Salt	5 g/ 1 tsp
Red chilli powder	5 g/ 1 tsp
Chopped ginger -	5 g/ 1 tsp

Heat the mustard oil in a pan until it smokes. Reduce the heat for about five minutes to allow the hot oil to cool off. Add in half the margosa leaves and when they begin to change color, add the diced eggplant, salt, chilli, and ginger. Simmer on low heat for about ten minutes, stirring occasionally until the eggplant has almost cooked through. Add in the remaining margosa leaves, cook a bit more, taste, and adjust the seasoning. Serve hot with steamed basmati rice.

Bengali Pumpkin and Eggplant Stew
Chor Chorri

This is probably one of the best vegetable stews I have ever had. When I say best, I speak of the balance of flavors, the contrast of textures, and the intermingling of spices that bring this taste sensation alive.

One of the primary appeals is the straight-forward honesty and simplicity of the dish. The commonly available ingredients and spices blend together to create magic.

Panch phoran is an Indian five-spice mix composed of equal quantities of cumin seeds, fennel, fenugreek, mustard and nigella (also known as kalonji).

Diced eggplant	150 g/ 3/4 cup
Diced pumpkin	200 g/ 1 cup
Diced white radish	150 g/ 3/4 cup
Spinach leaves, rinsed and trimmed	250 g/ 1 1/4 cup
Sugar or palm sugar	20 g/ 1 heaping tbsp
Dry red chillies	4
Panch phoran	5 g/ 1 tsp
Salt	to taste
Mustard oil	20 ml/ 1 tbsp
Turmeric powder	5 g/ 1 tsp

Heat the mustard oil in a heavy bottomed pan. When it smokes, reduce the heat and add the panch phoran. When the seeds crackle, add in the white radish, stir it around and add in the pumpkin, salt, and turmeric powder. Reduce the heat to a simmer and stir occasionally.

When the pumpkin begins to soften, add in the eggplant and continue to stir for ten minutes until the pumpkin and eggplant are soft. When the vegetables are almost done, taste, and adjust the seasoning, if required. Add in the sugar and spinach leaves.

Increase the heat and stir a few times to bring to heat. Serve hot with plain boiled rice.

Spinach Leaves with Ginger and Tomatoes

Adraki Palak

Spinach leaves	900 g/ 2 lbs
Oil	20 ml/ 1 tbsp
Mustard seeds	a pinch
Cumin seeds	a pinch
Chopped ginger	20 g/ 1 heaping tbsp
Chopped fresh chillies	10 g/ 2 tsp
Chopped tomatoes	100 g/ 1/2 cup
Salt	to taste
Roasted and lightly crushed coriander seeds	10 g/ 2 tsp
Juice of one lemon	

Wash the spinach leaves several times to ensure that the sand is washed away. Drain off the excess water and set aside.

Heat the oil in a heavy-bottomed pot and add the mustard and cumin seeds. When they crackle, add the ginger and chillies and stir on low heat for a bit until they turn soft. Add the tomatoes and simmer until they turn pulpy. Stir in the spinach leaves and salt and simmer until the spinach is soft. Sprinkle in the coriander seeds and lemon juice. Stir to mix well. Taste and adjust the seasonings, if required. Serve hot.

Spinach Leaves Tossed with Mustard
Sarson Palak

Spinach leaves, trimmed and rinsed	900 g/ 2 lbs
Mustard seeds	20 g/ 1 heaping tbsp
Green chillies	2
Turmeric powder	a pinch
Mustard oil	10 ml/ 2 tsp
Grated ginger	5 g/ 1 tsp
Salt-	to taste

Place the mustard seeds in a small bowl, cover them with hot water and set aside for fifteen minutes. In a food processor, grind the seeds to a coarse paste with the green chillies, and turmeric, adding water as might be necessary to make it into a paste.

Heat the oil in a pan until it smokes. Reduce the heat and add the mustard paste. Stir continuously on medium heat for about three minutes. Add the spinach leaves and salt, stir until the leaves wilt. Taste, and adjust the seasoning, if required. Serve hot with rice.

Okra Tossed with Spiced Yogurt
Dahi Bhindi

Tender okra	400g/ 2 cups
Mustard oil	20 ml/ 1 tbsp
Mustard seeds	a pinch
Curry leaves -	5 leaves
Asafoetida	a pinch
Turmeric powder	5 g/ 1 tsp
Chopped ginger	10 g/ 2 tsp
Chopped green chillies	5 g/ 1 tsp
Yogurt	200 g/ 1 cup
Salt	to taste
Chopped coriander leaves	5 g/ 1 tsp

Wash and pat the okra dry. Trim and discard the ends. Cut the leaves into inch-long pieces.

Heat the oil in a pan and fry the okra until they turn bright green. Remove with a slotted spoon and place on an absorbent kitchen paper towel to drain. Reheat the oil and add the mustard seeds, curry leaves, and asafoetida. When the seeds crackle, add the turmeric, ginger, green chillies, yogurt, and salt. Stir on low heat for a few minutes until the sauce begins to thicken and slide in the fried okra. Taste, and adjust the seasoning and spice, if required. Bring the sauce to a boil and sprinkle on the coriander leaves. Remove from heat and serve.

Okra Steamed with Yogurt and Spices

Dum Ki Bhindi

Okra	400g/ 2 cups
Carom seeds	a pinch
Chopped fresh chillies	10 g/ 2 tsp
Turmeric powder	5 g/ 1 tsp
Coriander powder	5 g/ 1 tsp
Yogurt	100 g/ 1/2 cup
Salt	to taste
Chopped fresh coriander	5 g/ 1 tsp

Wash and pat the okra dry and cut off their ends. Slice them in half lengthwise. Incorporate the carom seeds, chillies, turmeric, coriander, yogurt and salt. Set aside in a cool place for half an hour.

Heat a non-stick pan. Add the marinated okra mixture. Stir on high heat for a minute and then reduce the heat to a simmer. Cover and simmer for ten minutes, stirring occasionally. Taste and adjust the seasoning, if required. When the okra has cooked and most of the liquid has been absorbed, stir in the coriander leaves and remove the pan from the heat. Serve hot.

Okra with Spiced Baby Tomatoes
Khatta Bhindi

This dish of spiced and tangy okra is quite a favourite in the yogic community. Okra is a highly regarded vegetable because of its taste and health benefits. The traditional recipe calls for plump baby tomatoes, but I always add a bit of cherry tomato to make it a visually pleasant sensation as well.

Tender green okra	450 g/ 1 lb
Mustard oil	20 ml/ 1 tbsp
Cumin seeds	5 g/ 1 tsp
Chopped tomatoes	100 g/ ½ cup
Turmeric powder	5 g/ 1 tsp
Chopped fresh chillies	10 g/ 2 tsp
Chopped ginger	20 g/ 1 heaping tbsp
Cherry tomatoes cut in half	40 g/ 2 heaping tbsp
Salt	to taste
Lemon juice	10 ml/ 2 tsp
Chopped coriander leaves	5 g/ 1 tsp

Wash and pat the okra dry and trim them at both ends.

Heat the oil in a pan and fry the okra until they are bright green. Remove and drain on an absorbent kitchen paper towel. Reheat the same oil and add in the cumin seeds. When they crackle, add the tomatoes, turmeric powder, and fresh chillies. Cook until the tomatoes turn pulpy. Add the okra, ginger, cherry tomatoes, and salt and simmer for a few minutes until the sauces begin to coat the okra. Sprinkle on the lemon juice and coriander leaves. Stir, and adjust the seasonings, if required. Serve hot.

Stir Fried Cabbage with Mustard Seeds and Curry Leaves
Muttakos Poriyal

Chopped cabbage	400g/ 2 cups
Green peas	40 g/ 2 heaping tbsp
Oil	20 ml/ 1 tbsp

Mustard seeds	a pinch
Cumin seeds	a pinch
Split black lentils/ Udad dal	a pinch
Split Bengal gram/ chana dal	a pinch
Asafoetida powder	a pinch
Curry leaves	one sprig
Chopped green chillies	5 g/ 1 tsp
Grated coconut	40 g/ 2 heaping tbsp
Salt	to taste

Heat the oil in a pan and add the mustard and cumin seeds. When they crackle, add in the lentils, asafoetida, and curry leaves. Stir them on gentle heat until they change color. Add in the cabbage, peas, chillies, and salt. Stir until the vegetables soften. Taste and adjust seasoning, if required. Stir in the coconut. Serve hot.

Tomatoes Poached in a Spiced Tomato Sauce

Tamatar Ki Subzi

Certain cultures believe that the fabled fruit in the Garden of Eden was a tomato. That may have well been the case. I can imagine Eve would be willing to give up several comforts for a chance to sample this dish the way it was prepared for me.

Although this recipe calls for oven roasting the tomatoes, when I first ate them they were roasted on a coal fire, which gave them an absolutely exquisite earthy-smoky aroma.

Large tomatoes	400g/ 2 cups
Salt	to taste
Ghee	20 g/ 1 heaping tbsp
Mustard seeds	a pinch
Coriander seeds	a pinch
Fennel seeds	a pinch
Ground asafoetida	a pinch
Curry leaves	a sprig

Chopped fresh chillies	10 g/ 2 tsp
Gram flour/ Besan	40 g/ 2 heaping tbsp
Small tomatoes	600 g/ 1 ¼ lb
Chopped coriander leaves	10 g/ 2 tsp
Chopped mint leaves	5 g/ 1 tsp

Simmer the large tomatoes in a pot with 200 ml/ 1 cup of water and a pinch of salt. When the tomatoes are soft, puree them in a blender and pass through a strainer. Discard the skin and seeds.

Heat the ghee in a heavy-bottomed pot. Add the mustard, coriander, fennel seeds, and asafoetida until the spices crackle. Add the curry leaves, chillies, and gram flour. Stir on low heat until the flour turns golden. Add the pureed tomatoes and simmer on low heat for ten minutes.

Separately, roast the small tomatoes for two minutes in a hot oven. Remove and discard the skin. Slide these tomatoes into the sauce and bring it to a boil for less than a minute. Reduce the heat and simmer until the sauce thickens and is able to coat the back of a spoon. Taste and adjust seasonings, if required. Stir in the coriander and mint leaves. Serve hot.

Tomatoes Simmered in Coconut Milk

Tamaterachya Kodhi

Medium-sized tomatoes	600 g/ 3 cups
Oil	10 ml/ 2 tsp
Coconut oil	20 ml/ 1 tbsp
Mustard seeds	a pinch
Fenugreek	a pinch
Ground asafoetida	a pinch
Curry leaves	one sprig
Chopped ginger	10 g/ 2 tsp
Fresh chillies	10 g/ 2 tsp
Turmeric powder	10 g/ 2 tsp
Coconut milk	450 ml/ 2 ¼ cups
Salt	to taste
Chopped coriander leaves	10 g/ 2 tsp

| Desiccated or grated | |
| fresh coconut | 20 g/ 1 heaping tbsp |

Rub the tomatoes with oil and place them in a hot oven (160C/320F) for ten minutes. Peel off and discard the skin. Set the tomatoes aside.

Heat the coconut oil in a heavy-bottomed pot and add the mustard, fenugreek, asafoetida, and curry leaves. When the spices crackle, add the ginger, fresh chillies, turmeric, and coconut milk. Simmer for ten minutes. Slide the peeled tomatoes into the sauce along with salt and bring the sauce to a boil for just a minute. Reduce the heat and simmer until the sauce begins to coat the back of a spoon. Taste and adjust the seasonings, if necessary. Stir in the coriander leaves and coconut. Serve hot.

Spiced Cauliflower with Cumin Seeds

Gobi Jeera Masala

Cauliflower florets	300 g/ 2/3 lb
Ghee	20 g/ 1 heaping tbsp
Cumin seeds	a pinch
Shredded ginger	10 g/ 2 tsp
Chopped fresh chillies	5 g/ 1 tsp
Turmeric powder	5 g/ 1 tsp
Chilli powder	a pinch
Roughly chopped tomatoes	150 g/ 3/4 cup
Lime juice	5 ml
Chopped coriander leaves	5 g/ 1 tsp

Heat the ghee in a heavy-bottomed pot. Add the cumin seeds. When they crackle, add the cauliflower, ginger, fresh chillies, turmeric, and chilli powder. Simmer for a few minutes while stirring occasionally to prevent them from sticking to the bottom and burning. Add the tomatoes and simmer until they are pulpy. Taste and adjust the seasoning and spice levels, if required. When the cauliflower is done, remove from heat and stir in the lime juice and coriander leaves. Serve hot.

Kerala-Style Mixed Vegetable and Yogurt Stew

Avial

Drumstick, cut into inch long pieces, can be found in Indian food markets. Zucchini can be substituted. As drumstick is hardier, zucchini should be added at the end of the cooking)

Drumstick	100g
Yam, peeled and cut into 1- inch cubes–	100g
Runner beans cut into inch long pieces	100g
Green plantain thickly sliced	100g
White pumpkin, deseeded and cut into 1-inch cubes	100g
French beans, stringed and cut into inch long batons	100g
Grated coconut	100g
Coconut oil	75 ml/ 1/3 cup
Chopped shallots	40g/ 2 tbsp
Fresh chillies	10 g/ 2 tsp
Turmeric Powder	5 g/ 1 tsp
Cumin Seeds	a pinch
Beaten Yogurt	50 g/ ¼ cup
Curry Leaves	5 g/ 1 tsp
Salt	10 g/ 2 tsp
Sugar	5 g/ 1 tsp

Boil the vegetables in water with turmeric and a pinch of salt. Drain off the excess water well and set aside in a cool place.

Grind together the cumin seeds, grated coconut, fresh chillies and shallots to a coarse paste.

Heat half of the coconut oil, and add in the curry leaves. When they crackle, add the ground paste and the boiled vegetables.

Stir well, add in the beaten yogurt, and simmer for a few minutes.

Increase the heat to bring the mixture to a boil. Taste and adjust the seasoning, if required. Sprinkle in the sugar and drizzle the rest of the coconut oil on top. Remove from heat. Serve hot.

Sambhar

This is a traditional vegetable and spice gravy that has numerous variations. It is served all over South India. The vegetables and/or the spice components can be varied to suit the occasion or to complement the other dishes that will be served with it during the meal. The drumstick vegetable contributes to the goodness delivered to the body. I have included the traditional recipe for the spice powder although there are many commercial mixes available that can be used as a substitute. Although the recipe sounds tedious, it really isn't so. It becomes easier with practice.

For the powder

Coriander seeds	a pinch
Red chillies	3
Black peppercorns	a pinch
Cumin seeds	a pinch
Fenugreek seeds	a pinch
Mustard seeds	a pinch
Chana dal/ split Bengal gram	a pinch
Poppy seeds	a pinch
Grated coconut	5 g/ 1 tsp
Cinnamon stick	1
Curry leaves	one sprig

For the gravy

Drumstick can be found in Indian food markets or zucchini can be substituted. As drumstick is hardier, zucchini should be added at the end of the cooking.

Drumstick cut into batons	70 g/ 1/3 cup
Shallot–	50 g/ 1/4 cup
Potatoes peeled and cut into batons	50 g/ 1/4 cup
Radish (daikon),–	50 g/ 1/4 cup

Red pumpkin peeled and cut into 1- inch cubes	70 g/ 1/3 cup
Fresh chillies sliced in half lengthwise–	2
Sambhar powder	20 g/ 1 heaping tbsp
Turmeric powder	5 g/ 1 tsp
Tamarind pulp	20 g/ 1 heaping tbsp
Salt	to taste
Chopped coriander leaves	5 g/ 1 tsp

For the tempering

Oil	10 ml/ 2 tsp
Mustard seeds	a pinch
Asafoetida powder	a pinch
Cumin seeds	a pinch
Dried red chillies	2
Curry leaves	a sprig

Roast each ingredient for the powder individually. Grind them together to a fine powder. Set aside.

Boil about ½ quart/litre of water with the turmeric powder, salt, fresh chillies, tamarind pulp, and sambhar spice powder. Add in all of the vegetables. Simmer until the vegetables are almost done and the gravy has started to thicken.

Separately heat the oil and add the ingredients for the tempering. When the seeds splutter, swirl them around in the hot oil a few times and pour this over the sambhar. Stir the stew a few times until the seasonings are blended. taste and adjust the seasoning, if required. Sprinkle on the coriander leaves. Serve hot.

Rustic Chickpea Curry

Choley Masala

Chickpeas	200 g/ 1 cup
Carom seeds/ Ajwain	5 g/ 1 tsp
Salt	to taste

Cardamom pods	4
Cinnamon stick	2
Bay leaves	2
Cloves	4
Coriander seeds	a pinch
Oil	20 ml
Cumin seeds	a pinch
Asafoetida	5 g/ 1 tsp
Tomatoes	150 g/ 3/4 cup
Chopped fresh chillies	10 g/ 2 tsp
Chopped ginger	10 g/ 2 tsp
Turmeric powder	10 g/ 2 tsp
Chopped fresh coriander	5 g/ 1 tsp
Juice of one lemon	

Wash the chickpeas well and soak them overnight with the carom seeds and a bit of salt. Drain off the water and wash a few more times.

Gently crush the cardamom, cinnamon, bay leaves, cloves and coriander seeds. Tie them in a piece of cheesecloth and boil in water along with the beans until the beans become soft.

Heat the oil in a heavy-bottomed pot and add in the cumin and asafoetida. When the seeds begin to change color, add the tomatoes and cook on medium heat until they are pulpy. Add the boiled chickpeas along with the remaining liquid, chillies, ginger, turmeric, and salt. Stir a few times. Mash some of the beans in the pot to give the sauce thickness. Taste and adjust the seasoning and spice levels, if required. Stir in the coriander and lemon juice. Serve hot.

Red Kidney Bean and Yogurt Stew

Dahiwale Rajmah

Red kidney beans	300 g/ 1 ½ cup
Ghee	20 g/ 1 heaping tbsp
Coriander seeds	5 g/ 1 tsp
Carom seeds/ ajwain	5 g/ 1 tsp
Chopped onions	70 g/ 1/3 cup

Chopped garlic	10 g/ 2 tsp
Chopped ginger	10 g/ 2 tsp
Chopped fresh chillies	20 g/ 1 heaping tbsp
Chopped tomatoes	100 g/ 1/2 cup
Salt	to taste
Yogurt	150 g/ 3/4 cup
Chopped coriander leaves	20 g/ 1 heaping tbsp

Wash the kidney beans. Let them soak in water and set aside in a cool place for three hours.

Heat the ghee in a heavy-bottomed pot. Add the coriander and carom seeds. When they splutter and begin to change color, add the onions. Stir on medium heat until they are golden. Add in the garlic and continue to cook until the garlic changes color. Add in the ginger, chillies, and tomatoes. Simmer on medium heat until the tomatoes are soft and pulpy. Drain the kidney beans and add them to the pot with a bit of salt and 500 ml/ 2 ½ cups of water. Simmer the beans. Stir occasionally until they are soft. This should take about a half hour.

Whip the yogurt until it is smooth and add it to the pot. Mix well. Increase the heat, bringing the beans to a rapid boil. Taste and adjust seasonings. if required. Remove form heat and mix in the coriander leaves. Serve hot.

Tempered Lentils with Cumin and Mustard

Tadkewalli Dal

Red lentils/ Masoor dal	50 g/ 1/4 cup
Cumin seeds	a pinch
Clarified butter/ Ghee	5 g/ 1 tsp
Slit green chilli	1 piece
Turmeric powder	a pinch
Salt	to taste
Oil	5 ml
Chopped fresh chillies	5 g/ 1 tsp
Mustard seeds	a pinch
Chopped coriander leaves	a pinch

Wash the lentils in running water and drain.

In a heavy-bottomed pot, heat the ghee and add in the cumin seeds. When the seeds crackle, add in the lentils and stir them in the pot until they are opaque. Add the turmeric powder, the salt and the slit green chilli. Stir for two more minutes and then add about 300 ml/ 1 ½ cups of water.

Reduce the heat and simmer the lentils until they are soft and mashed. Taste and adjust the seasoning, if required.

In a pan, heat the oil and add in the mustard seeds and chopped fresh chillies. When the seeds crackle, pour the oil-spice mixture over the lentils. Finish with the chopped coriander leaves. Serve hot.

Paneer

Paneer, or what Indians call cottage cheese, is probably the only indigenous cheese known to the Asian region. It is not the crumbly, liquidy cheese that is called cottage cheese in the United States. It has the texture of a very soft, freshly made mozzarella. Unlike mozzarella, it is unique in that it does not melt at regular cooking temperatures. It is not aged, used fresh, and because the milk is split into curds and whey using acid (lime), not rennet, it is truly a vegetarian cheese.

Paneer is made from milk which is split using acid as the agent. The resultant coagulated protein masses are collected and pressed in a mold with a weight on them to cause them to stick together to form a block. This block can then be sliced or cut into cubes depending on the dish in which you wish to use them.

Often a softer version of this cheese is prepared for which pressing does not take place. Instead, the cheese is kneaded to form a fluffier, softer cheese which is used in the preparation of desserts.

Although paneer is "Indian," it was made popular by the Mughal invaders who ruled over most of India during the Middle Ages. It is an unsalted cheese that readily accepts flavors and stands up to prolonged marinating. It absorbs the flavors of the dish it is used in, so prior marinating with salt is unnecessary.

Paneer is the primary source of protein for those Indian vegetarians who adhere to a strict lacto-vegetarian diet.

It is easy to make at home and often available Asian groceries.

Homemade Paneer

I often come across those who shrug off the idea of purchasing factory-prepared paneer as being too modern and the cheese having no taste. Nothing can truly replace the fresh, creamy texture of homemade and home-pressed paneer. Although the method initially takes a bit of time, it becomes quick and simple after a bit of experience. The procedure has not changed since those ancient times when civilization first discovered the method for making cheese.

Because the cheese is created by the retention of only the milk solids and fats while discarding of the residual liquid, the yield tends to be low. The following recipe yields about 200 g/ or 1 cup of finished paneer. For variation, you might consider introducing such things as carom seeds or turmeric powder to the milk.

Whole milk	1 litre/ 1 quart
Lime juice	40 ml/ 2 tbsp

Bring the milk to a boil, continually stirring gently to prevent it from burning and sticking to the bottom of the pot. When at a boil, remove it from the heat. Pour in the lemon juice slowly while stirring at all times. (Indians use the words lemon and lime equivalently as yellow lemons are rarely seen in India.) When the milk curdles, and the solid matter has floated to the top, stop stirring and allow it to stand for about fifteen minutes. Drain through a fine muslin or cheese cloth, retaining the solid matter. Squeeze a few times to remove excess liquid and wrap it thoroughly, placing it on a flat surface with a weight on it so residual liquid will be pressed out and continues to drain away. A bowl or pot filled with water makes a good weight. Be sure its bottom surface covers the entire block.

After half an hour, remove off the weight, unwrap the cheese and cut into desired pieces.

Although this cheese is best used immediately, it keeps well under refrigeration for three to five days.

Paneer and Green Peas Simmered in Creamy Spinach Gravy

Palak Matar Paneer

Spinach leaves, rinsed clean	450 g/ 1 lb
Shredded ginger	5 g/ 1 tsp
Chopped fresh chilli	1
Cumin seeds –	a pinch
Turmeric powder	a pinch
Paneer cut into cubes	50 g/ ¼ cup
Green peas	50 g/ ¼ cup
Red chilli powder –	5 g/ 1 tsp
Oil	10 ml/ 2 tsp

Cream	20 ml/ 1 tbsp
Salt	to taste
Ghee/ clarified butter	5 g/ 1 tsp

In a pot, boil the spinach with some salt, the ginger, the fresh chilli, and the turmeric powder. When soft, drain off the excess water and cool the spinach under cold, running water to retain the color. Puree the spinach in a food processor.

In a heavy-bottomed pot, heat some oil and add the cumin seeds. When the seeds crackle, add the ground spinach and stir over high heat. Continue stirring until the spinach begins to thicken and appears almost dry. Add in the cream, the chilli powder, paneer cubes, green peas, and a bit of salt. Reduce the heat to simmer.

After a few minutes, taste and adjust the seasoning. When the gravy begins to bubble and is thick and creamy, remove from the heat. Serve hot.

Crumbled Paneer with Spices

Paneer Bhurji

I have always maintained that this recipe is possibly the best treatment ever devised for paneer. With its unique texture and taste, paneer lends this simple dish a twist of versatility, ease, and uniqueness that would probably not work with any other base ingredient.

Paneer, grated	300 g/ 1 ½ cup
Oil	20 ml/ 1 tbsp
Cumin seeds	a pinch
Chopped onions	50 g/ ¼ cup
Chopped fresh chillies	10 g/ 2 tsp
Turmeric powder	10 g/ 2 tsp
Chopped tomatoes	50 g/ ¼ cup
Salt	to taste
Chopped coriander leaves	5 g/ 1 tsp
Juice of one lemon	

Heat the oil in a pan and add the cumin seeds. When they crackle, add in the chopped onions and fresh chillies. Stir on medium heat until the onions are soft. Add the paneer, turmeric powder, and salt. Continue to stir to prevent the spices from sticking to the bottom and burning. Add the tomatoes and simmer them until they are pulpy. Taste and adjust the seasoning, if necessary. Finish with chopped coriander leaves and sprinkle on the lemon juice. Serve hot.

Breads

Unleavened Griddle-Cooked Bread
Chappati

Chappati, also known as phulka because it puffs up during cooking, is a traditional, unleavened, home-cooked bread. The use of unprocessed whole wheat flour makes it nutritious. If desired, one may even forego adding oil to the dough. It is generally eaten with dinner because it is light and easily digested.

Whole wheat flour	300 g/ 1 ½ cup
Oil	20 ml/ 1 tbsp
Salt	to taste

Sift the flour with salt, remove approximately 25 g/ 1 tsp/ of flour and set it aside for dusting. Add the oil and about 180 ml/ ¾ cups of water to the flour and knead it until it forms a soft dough. Separate the dough into even, round, lemon-sized balls and leave them to rest for half an hour covered with a damp kitchen towel.

Roll the balls into flat discs and toast them on moderate heat on a griddle or in a non-stick pan, flipping occasionally until they are evenly golden and baked. Serve hot.

Traditional Whole Wheat and Carom Seed Griddle-Cooked Bread
Ajwaini Paratha

Whole wheat flour	300 g/ 1 ½ cup
Salt	to taste
Carom seeds	5 g/ 1 tsp
Ghee	40 g/ 2 generous tbsp
Water	as required

Sift the flour with the salt. Remove about 20 g/ 1 tbsp of flour and keep aside for dusting. Melt the ghee and add half of it to the flour along with the carom seeds. Gently mix the ghee with the flour until the flour becomes crumbly. Add in enough water (roughly about 150 ml/ ¾ cup) to knead to a soft dough. Divide the dough and form it into lemon-sized balls. Cover with a damp kitchen towel and set aside for about twenty minutes.

Roll the dough out flat, into whatever shape it becomes. Brush with a bit of ghee, and dust some flour over the surface. Beginning from one end, pleat the dough into gathered folds as one would alternately pleat a paper fan. Roll from one end to the other so that it now resembles a slice of jelly roll. Place the loose end under the dough and do the same to the remaining balls of dough. Set aside to rest for about fifteen minutes before rolling them again into round discs with roughly half an inch of thickness.

Toast them on moderate heat on a griddle or in a non-stick pan, flipping occasionally until they are evenly golden and baked. Brush with a bit of ghee and continue until they are baked. Serve hot.

Beetroot and Cardamom Bread

Chukandar Ki Roti

Beetroots are healthy, nutritious, and a good source of fiber. The tender shoots are eaten during the summer and the beet itself is best eaten during the winter. Because they are easy to grow, harvests are generally abundant. They can be pickled, dried, or salted to facilitate storage.

Beetroot	200 g/ 1 cup
Cardamom	10 pods
Whole wheat flour	400g/ 2 cups
Oil	20 ml/ 1 tbsp
Chopped ginger	10 g/ 2 tsp
Salt	to taste
Ghee	10 g/ 2 tsp

Boil the beetroot for twenty minutes to soften them. Peel and then puree them in a blender. Pound the cardamom in a mortar with a pestle or pulse them in a food processor until they are a coarse powder. Pick out and discard the shells and add the powder to the beetroot puree.

Mix the flour, oil, ginger, salt, and pureed beets. Knead the mixture thoroughly to form a soft, smooth dough. Divide the dough into lemon-sized balls. Cover with a damp cloth and rest them in a cool place for half an hour.

Sprinkle a bit of flour onto a board and roll the dough balls into flat round discs. Toast them on moderate heat on a griddle or in a non-stick pan, flipping occasionally until they are evenly golden and baked. Brush a bit of the ghee onto each bread. Serve hot.

Sorghum Bread
Jwarichi Bhakri

Sorghum is a rather hard grain grown abundantly in Maharashtra. This bread is a poor man's food nourishing enough to make up for the deficiencies of a poor diet.

Sorghum flour (jawar as it is colloquially known) is available at most Indian grocers.

Jawar flour/Sorghum flour	450 g/ 1 lb
Water (approximately)	200 ml/ 1 cup
Salt	10 g/ 2 tsp
Butter or ghee (Optional)	20 g/ 1 heaping tbsp

Knead together the flour, salt, and enough water to make a soft smooth dough. Divide the dough into lemon-sized balls. Flatten the balls with your palms into flat, round discs, about a third of an inch thick. Toast them on moderate heat on a griddle or in a non-stick pan, flipping occasionally until they are evenly golden and baked. Brush on the butter or ghee. Serve hot.

Spiced Chickpea Flour Bread
Missi Roti

Gram flour	250 g/ 1 1/4 cup
Whole wheat flour	150 g/ 3/4 cup
Red chilli powder	5 g/ 1 tsp
Chopped green chillies	2
Oil	20 ml/ 1 tbsp

Bishops weed/ajwain	a pinch
Turmeric powder	a pinch
Salt	to taste
Ghee	20 g/ 1 tbsp

Mix together the whole gram flour, the whole wheat flour, red chilli powder, turmeric powder, green chillies, ajwain, and salt. Add in the oil and enough water to knead into a soft, smooth dough.

Divide the dough into lemon sized balls. With a rolling pin, roll each ball into a round, flat 4-inch disc. Toast them on moderate heat on a griddle or in a non-stick pan, flipping occasionally until they are evenly golden and baked. Brush with ghee. Serve hot.

Fenugreek Flavored Flat Bread
Methi Na Thepla

Finely chopped fenugreek leaves/ methi patta	50 g/ 1/4 cup
Whole wheat flour/ atta	200 g/ 1 cup
Roasted cumin seeds powdered	a pinch
Turmeric powder	a pinch
Finely chopped coriander leaves	10 g/ 2 tsp
Red chilli powder	5 g/ 1 tsp
Salt	to taste
Oil for kneading	40 ml/ 2 tbsp
Ghee for basting	20 g/ 1 heaping tbsp

Knead together the fenugreek leaves, whole wheat flour, powdered cumin, turmeric powder, coriander leaves, chilli powder, salt, oil, and enough water to make a smooth, soft dough.

Divide the dough into lemon-sized balls and roll them into ¼-inch thin disc shapes. Heat a griddle or non-stick pan on moderate heat and toast the dough on both sides until it begins to turn golden. Brush on a bit of the ghee and cook further on both sides until golden and done. Serve warm or at room temperature with a sweet mango chutney.

Fried Bread with Split Black Lentils
Urad Dal Kachori

For the mixture

Urad dal soaked for half an hour	125 g/ 5/8 cup
Mustard oil	20 ml/ 1 tbsp
Fennel seeds/ saunf	a pinch
Chopped ginger	a pinch
Asafoetida	a pinch
Cumin seeds	a pinch
Salt	to taste

For the dough

Refined (white) flour/ maida	200 g/ 1 cup
Semolina/ sooji	150 g/ 3/4 cup
Melted ghee	20 g/ 1 heaping tbsp
Water	approximately 200 ml/ 1 cup to start
Salt	5 g/ 1 tsp
Vegetable oil	for frying

Drain the lentils and, adding water if needed, grind them to a paste in a food processor along with the ginger and fennel. In a heavy-bottomed pan, heat the oil and fry the asafoetida until it is golden. Add the cumin seeds. When they crackle add the lentil paste. Cook the mixture until it is thick. The final result should be like soft clay. Remove from heat and let cool. Divide into lemon-sized balls.

For the dough, sift the flour with the salt. Mix in the ghee and the semolina. Knead until achieving a crumbly texture. Add in the water slowly and continue to knead for about ten more minutes until the dough is soft in texture. Add small amounts of water or flour, as required, to adjust the texture of the dough. Divide into a dozen lemon-sized balls and set them aside to rest in a cool place for fifteen minutes.

Place a dough ball in the center of your palm and flatten it a bit. Cup your hands so that the dough forms a pouch. Place a ball of the lentil mixture in the center and envelope it with the dough. Roll the dough in your hand to seal the opening and form a ball. Roll each dough ball into thin round discs making sure that they do not tear and the filling does not come out. Heat the oil in a wok or a deep round-bottomed pan. Slide the discs into the hot oil. Turn them over when they puff up. Fry on both sides until they are equally golden. Serve hot.

Traditional Whole Wheat Flour Fried Bread

Poori

Whole wheat flour	450 g/ 1 lb
Melted ghee	20 g/ 1 heaping tbsp
Salt	10 g/ 2 tsp
Water	300 ml/ 1 ½ cup
Oil for rolling the dough	10 ml/ 2 tsp
Oil for deep-frying	

Sift the flour with the salt. Mix the flour thoroughly with the melted ghee until it achieves a crumbly texture. Mix in the water and knead well for ten to twelve minutes. Adjust the flour or water, as necessary, to make a firm dough. Form the dough into lemon-sized balls and let rest for fifteen minutes. Use a rolling pin to roll the balls into flat evenly shaped discs of less than 1/8-inch thickness. Dabbing a bit of oil on the dough will facilitate rolling. Heat the oil in a fryer or-round bottomed wok. When hot, slide the discs in one at a time. When they puff up, turn them over and fry both sides until they are evenly golden. Serve hot.

Rice

Ever since the first rice grains were domesticated, they have been a source of sustenance as well as an enigma. It has been described in ancient mythology as both a boon from the gods and a gift from the earth to thank men for their labors. It is mentioned in ancient Vedic texts, in medical treatises like the *Sushrutha Samitha* and the *Charaka Samitha*, and even carved into the ancient Pramban temples of Java.

When rice became a domesticated crop over six thousand years ago, few would have realized the prominence to which this grain would be raised—such as to command armies and conquests, influence foreign policies, and generally affect the lifestyle and eating habits of more than half of the world's population.

In India, rice holds even religious importance. Newlyweds are showered with rice grains to promote fertility; rice is used in several religious ceremonies to indicate prosperity; and babies are fed rice as part of their first solid meals.

The reason for the great success of rice is its amazing ability to grow in most terrains. It is well-suited to the wet, long monsoons that major areas of Southeast Asia endure. Rice farming and its harvesting is heavily labor intensive (a reason why its cultivation has not spread around the globe).

In India, where thousands of varieties of rice are grown, the Basmati variety reigns supreme. This is not because it is a clearly superior strain of rice but the result of subtle and well-played marketing methods.

When the Mughal Empire overran most of the central and north- west of the sub-continent, they demanded tithes and tributes. Rice was always available aplenty and plans were hatched by the rulers of the smaller principalities to get off lightly. Basmati was touted as a gift from the gods, poets waxed lyrical about its goodness, and story tellers carried tales filled with the excitement and adventure of Basmati everywhere they went.

Sure enough, the rice was made a part of the tribute that was required to be placed before the royal thrones.

Basmati is a wonderful, long-grained rice with a subtle fragrance. Its lower starch content ensures that the grains do not stick to each other. However, there are several thousand other varieties, each with their own personalities and attributes.

The use of a particular strain of rice in Indian cooking has more to do with economic and regional factors than do those of taste. Basmati has always been thought of as a premium rice and was thus used for celebratory feasts. The Bengalis swear by the short-grained, locally grown *Gobindobhog*, a strain that is generally unknown to those outside of their community.

Farmers in rural communities often eat the healthier unpolished rice, having had only the husk removed. More expensive milled rice is reserved for city dwellers who can afford the additional processing charges.

The harvesting of rice is done mainly by hand. The seeds are hulled using a machine called a rice huller that strips off the chaff, the outer husks of the grain. The grains then get milled further to polish off the bran and they become eye-pleasing pearly white grains. They are then often rolled in some form of powdered starch to give them a shiny appearance.

Brown rice is probably one of the healthier grains, but it does not have a lengthy shelf life and is thus not much available commercially.

Parboiled rice is a bit more nutritious. Parboiling takes place before the milling, transferring the nutrients onto the grain itself.

Rice must be washed several times before cooking it to remove all traces of starch. This rule does not apply to those companies that offer a fortified variety of rice of which they warn that washing the grain will result in the loss of those added nutrients.

The two most common methods of preparing rice remain the steaming method and the boiling method, although my travels have introduced me to raw vegans and fruitarians who sprout the grains as a grass, a process that takes about two weeks.

Commercially available rice cookers have eliminated much of the stress and overcooking attendant to the steaming method. The traditional method advises simmering the grains in twice their amount of salted water until all of the liquid had been absorbed and the rice grains appear fluffy.

The boiling method is used by a majority of Indians. The washed rice grains are put into ten times their amount of salted, boiling water. The grains, depending on their type, should take from twelve to fifteen minutes to soften. All of the liquid is drained, retaining only the cooked grains of rice. Water is often poured over the finished rice to stop its cooking and eliminate the remainder of starch.

Rice being a rather neutral-flavored grain tends to absorb and enhance external flavors. This works really well when flavoring rice or serving it with a highly flavored curry. Adding some whole spices like cardamom, cinnamon and/or cloves to the water when boiling or steaming the rice tends to enhance its taste.

Many of my recipes may call for Basmati rice; please substitute with any rice that you might prefer. A point worth noting is that the amount of water should be adjusted according to the type of rice being prepared.

Date Pilaf
Khajoor ka Pulao

Raw rice (preferably long grained Basmati)	400g/ 2 cups
Ghee	40 g/ 2 heaping tbsp
Cardamom pods	4
Cloves	6
Cinnamon	1 stick
Fennel seeds	a pinch
Chopped seedless dates	40 g/ 2 heaping tbsp
Chopped fresh chillies	20 g/ 1 heaping tbsp
Shredded ginger	20 g/ 1 heaping tbsp
Salt	to taste
Mint leaves	10 g/ 2 tsp

Wash the rice several times until the grains are free of most of the starch. Cover the rice with water and let it soak for ten minutes.

Heat the ghee in a pot and add the cardamom, cloves, cinnamon, and fennel. When the spices begin to puff up and change color, add the drained rice grains and stir over medium heat until they turn opaque. Add the dates, fresh chillies, ginger, and salt. Stir for a few minutes. Pour in about 600 ml/ 3 cups of water, cover the pot and simmer for about twenty minutes or until the water is absorbed and the rice is tender. Remove from the hat and stir in the mint leaves. Serve hot.

Tamarind Rice

Imliwaale Pulao

Rice	400g/ 2 cups
Ghee	20 g/ 1 heaping tbsp
Mace	2
Cinnamon	2 sticks
Cardamom	5 pods
Ginger	20 g/ 1 heaping tbsp
Fresh chillies	10 g/ 2 tsp
Tamarind pulp	50 ml/ ¼ cup
Sugar	a pinch
Salt	to taste
Chopped coriander leaves	10 g/ 2 tsp
Chopped mint leaves	5 g/ 1 tsp

Risne the rice several times until all of the starch has been washed away. Soak in water for ten minutes. Drain the excess water and discard it.

Heat the ghee in a pot and add the mace, cinnamon, and cardamom. When the spices begin to swell and change color, add the ginger, chillies, and drained rice. Sstir until the rice appears opaque. Add the tamarind pulp, sugar, salt, and 700 ml/ 3 ½ cups of water. Simmer covered for twenty minutes. Stir occasionally until all of the water has been absorbed and the rice is cooked through and fluffy. Mix in the coriander and tamarind leaves. Serve hot.

Sprouted Bean Pilaf

Ankurit Moong ka Pulao

Beansprouts	150 g/ 3/4 cup
Rice	400g/ 2 cups
Ghee	40 g/ 2 heaping tbsp
Cumin seeds	a pinch
Cardamom pods	6
Cinnamon stick	2
Bay leaves	4

Cloves	4
Chopped fresh chillies	20 g/ 1 heaping tbsp
Chopped ginger	20 g/ 1 heaping tbsp
Salt	to taste
Lemon juice	20 ml/ 1 tbsp
Chopped coriander leaves	10 g/ 2 tsp

Rinse the rice until all of the starch washes away. Soak the rice in water for about ten minutes. Drain the excess water and discard it.

Heat the ghee in a heavy-bottomed pot and add the cumin, cardamom, cinnamon, bay leaves and cloves. When the spices crackle, begin to swell and change color, add the drained rice and stir until they appear opaque. Add the chillies, ginger, and a bit of salt. Stir for a few more minutes. Pour in about 700 ml/ 3 ½ cups of water and bring it to a boil. Add in the sprouted beans, salt, and reduce the heat. Cover the pot and simmer for about twenty minutes until all of the water is absorbed and the rice is tender. Stir in the lemon juice and coriander leaves. Serve hot.

Sprouted Moong Bean and Red (Brown) Rice Pilaf

Tirangi Pulao

Brown rice	450 g/ 1 lb
Sprouted moong beans or use beansprouts	100 g/ ½ cup packed tight
Oil	20 ml/ 1 tbsp
Cumin seeds	a pinch
Green cardamom pods	4
Cloves	4 buds
Cinnamon stick	1
Bay leaf	1
Chopped onions	50 g/ ¼ cup
Shredded ginger	10 g/ 2 tsp
Chopped tomatoes	50 g/ ¼ cup
Chopped fresh chillies	5 g/ 1 tsp

Salt	to taste
Grated fresh or desiccated coconut	50 g/ 1/4 cup
Chopped coriander leaves	5 g/ 1 tsp
Juice of one lemon	

Rinse the rice several times until the water runs clear. Let it soak in water for about thirty minutes. Drain away the excess water. Boil the rice in 5 cups of salted water for thirty minutes until it is cooked three quarters of the way.

Heat the oil in a heavy-bottomed pot and add the cumin seeds, cardamom, cloves, cinnamon, and bay leaf. When the spices begin to swell and change color, stir in the onions on low heat until they turn transparent. Add the bean sprouts and continue to stir for about five minutes, until they are soft. Add salt, ginger, tomatoes, green chillies, 50 ml/ ¼ cup of water, and the rice. Simmer until the rice is tender and all the liquid has evaporated. Mix in the coconut, coriander leaves, and lemon juice. Serve hot.

Red (Brown) Rice Cooked with Spices and Garbanzo Beans

Channa Pulao

During that time when I was living at the hermitage, farmers occasionally dropped off enormous bundles of freshly harvested red [called brown in the U.S.] rice as offerings and tokens of their gratitude. My fervor would almost hit feverish pitch. I knew what would come next and what was expected of me. After I had threshed the grain, winnowed and discarded the chaff, parboiled the rice and spread the grains out for two days in the sun to dry, I could look forward to this amazingly fragrant and nutritious pilaf.

Brown rice	400g/ 2 cups
Chickpeas (or equivalent of canned garbanzos)	100 g/ 1/2 cup
Ghee	40 g/ 2 heaping tbsp
Cardamom	5 pods
Mace	2
Star anise	5
Cinnamon	2 sticks
Chopped tomatoes	100 g/ 1/2 cup

Chopped ginger	10 g/ 2 tsp
Chopped fresh chillies	20 g/ 1 heaping tbsp
Turmeric powder	10 g/ 2 tsp
Salt	to taste
Chopped coriander leaves	10 g/ 2 tsp
Juice of one lemon	

Rinse the rice until water runs clear. Boil in five cups of hot salted water for twenty-five minutes until it is almost cooked through. Drain. Spread the rice on a large tray to allow it to cool rapidly (allowing to cool in a bowl would permit the centers to continue to cook).

Soak the chickpeas in hot water for half an hour and then boil them in salted water for an hour until they are almost done (or use canned).

Heat the ghee in a heavy-bottomed pot. Add the cardamom, mace, star anise, and cinnamon. When the spices change color, add the drained rice, chickpeas, tomatoes, ginger, chillies, turmeric, and salt. Stir on medium heat for about five minutes. When the tomatoes turn pulpy, add 50 ml/ ¼ cup of water and simmer until all ofthe liquid has been absorbed.

Mix in the coriander, mint, and lemon juice without breaking the rice grains. Serve hot.

Red (Brown) Rice and Lentil Kedgeree
Laal Chawal Khichadi

Many sages and yogis live on a diet of khichadi. This rice and lentil mash need not be monotonous because the prime ingredients (like the type of rice or lentils) can be varied and a variety of vegetables added, depending on the occasion, the season, or availability.

Because red rice takes a longer time to cook, Ama, the wife of the guru, who was also the chef in the hermitage, would set out all the ingredients in a pot on the coal embers so that it cooked throughout the night. She mixed the vegetables into it in the morning and served it to us for breakfast.

While the smokiness provide by cooking over coal embers adds a special something to the dish, I have had great (and faster) results using a modern pressure cooker.

Red rice	400g/ 2 cups
Red kidney beans	100 g/ 1/2 cup
Split mung lentils/ dhuli mung dal	125 g/ 5/8 cup
Ghee	20 g/ 1 heaping tbsp
Asafoetida powder	10 g/ 2 tsp
Cumin seeds	5 g/ 1 tsp
Chopped fresh chillies	20 g/ 1 heaping tbsp
Chopped ginger	20 g/ 1 heaping tbsp
Chopped tomatoes	100 g/ 1/2 cup
Turmeric powder	20 g/ 1 heaping tbsp
Mint leaves	40 g/ 2 heaping tbsp
Coriander leaves	50 g/ 1/4 cup
Salt	to taste
Green peas	50 g/ 1/4 cup
Chopped coriander leaves	10 g/ 2 tsp
Juice of one lemon	

Rinse the rice several times until the water runs clear. Let soak in water for about thirty minutes. Rinse and then soak the kidney beans and lentils separately for three hours.

Heat the ghee in a heavy-bottomed pot. Add the asafoetida and cumin seeds. When they crackle and begin to change color, add them and the fresh chillies, ginger, and tomatoes to the drained rice, beans, and lentils. Stir occasionally. Simmer for twenty minutes until the tomatoes are pulpy.

Grind together the turmeric, mint, and coriander in a food processor, adding some water if necessary to get a thick paste. Add this paste to the rice with salt and a liter/5 cups of water. Simmer the rice covered for a further half hour, stirring occasionally until the liquid has been absorbed and the rice and lentils are cooked through. Stir in the green peas and simmer until they are cooked through. Stir in the lemon juice and coriander leaves and remove from heat. Serve hot.

Beetroot and Cumin Pilaf

Chukandar Pulao

Raw beetroot, peeled and chopped	200 g/ 1 cup
Rice (uncooked)	450 g/ 1 lb
Mustard seeds	10 g/ 2 tsp
Fresh chillies	10 g/ 2 tsp
Oil	20 ml/ 1 tbsp
Cumin seeds	5 g/ 1 tsp
Chopped onions	40 g/ 2 heaping tbsp
Chopped ginger	20 g/ 1 heaping tbsp
Salt	to taste
Chopped coriander leaves	5 g/ 1 tsp

Soak the mustard seeds in hot water for about a half hour. In a food processor, grind to a thick paste along with the fresh chillies.

Heat the oil in a heavy-bottomed pot and add the cumin seeds. When they crackle, add the chopped onions and cook them gently until they are golden. Add the beetroot, rice, and ground mustard paste. Cook on medium heat until the beetroot begins to soften. Add ginger, salt, and about 850 ml/ 4 cups of water. Cover and simmer the rice until done. Remove from heat. Gently stir in the coriander leaves without mashing the rice. Serve hot with an optional drizzle of ghee.

Cinnamon and Raisin Pilaf

Kaala Pulao

Rice	450 g/ 1 lb
Ghee	20 g/ 1 heaping tbsp
Cinnamon sticks	4
Star anise	3
Raisins	40 g/ 2 heaping tbsp
Chopped tomatoes	100 g/ ½ cup
Ginger	20 g/ 1 heaping tbsp

Crushed black peppercorns	10 g/ 2 tsp
Palm or cane sugar	20 g/ 1 heaping tbsp
Fennel seeds	5 g/ 1 tsp
Mint leaves	5 g/ 1 tsp
Salt	to taste

Rinse the rice until it runs clear. Drain. Heat the ghee in a heavy-bottomed pot. Add the cinnamon, star anise, and raisins. When the spices change color, add in the rice and stir until it becomes translucent. Add the tomatoes, ginger, peppercorns, sugar, and a bit of salt. Stir on medium heat until the tomatoes brown (well, not actually "brown," but become pulpy and carmelized). Add about 850 ml/ 4 cups of water, cover the pot and simmer for about twenty minutes, until the rice is done.

Broil the fennel seeds in a dry pan and pound them coarsely in a mortar with a pestle. Stir the fennel seeds into the rice along with the mint leaves. Serve hot.

Raisin and Paneer Pilaf

Murwa Pulao

Raisins	100 g/ 1/2 cup
Paneer cut into cubes	100 g/ ½ cup
Rice	400g/ 2 cups
Ghee	20 g/ 1 tbsp
Fennel seeds	a pinch
Cardamom pods	5
Cloves	5
Cinnamon	1 stick
Star anise	4
Bay leaves	2
Sliced shallots	100 g/ ½ cup
Chopped ginger	20 g/ 1 heaping tbsp
Turmeric powder	10 g/ 2 tsp
Salt	to taste
Chopped mint leaves	5 g/ 1 tsp
Chopped coriander leaves	5 g/ 1 tsp

Rinse the rice several times until the water runs clear. Let soak in water for about thirty minutes.

Heat the ghee in a heavy-bottomed pot and add the fennel, cardamom, cloves, cinnamon, star anise, and bay leaves. When the spices begin to change color, add the shallots and stir them on medium heat until they are golden. Add the raisins, paneer, and rice and continue to stir until the rice grains appear opaque. Add the ginger, turmeric powder, and a bit of salt. Stir for a few minutes and add about 700 ml/ 3 ½ cups of water. Reduce to a simmer. Cook covered for approximately 20-25 minutes, until the liquid has been absorbed and the rice is cooked. Mix in the mint and coriander. Remove from heat. Serve hot.

Cumin-flavored Rice

Jeera pulao

Special occasions can call for fragrant rice that compliments the richness and spice of the main courses. This is a really easy dish to prepare. It delivers fantastic results.

Rice	600 g/ 3 cups
Ghee	20 ml/ 1 tbsp
Cumin seeds	5 g/ 1 tsp
Cardamom pods	4
Cinnamon stick	1
Chopped onions	50 g/ ¼ cup
Salt	to taste
Chopped coriander leaves	10 g/ 2 tsp

Rinse the rice several times until the water runs clear. Let soak in water for about thirty minutes.

Heat the ghee in a heavy-bottomed pot and add the cumin, cardamom, and cinnamon. When the spices begin to change color, add the onions and simmer on medium heat until they are golden. Add the rice and continue to stir until the grains turn opaque. [opaque, translucent?] Add salt and a litre/ quart of water. Reduce the heat to a simmer and cook covered until the liquid is absorbed and the rice is done. Stir in the coriander leaves. Serve hot.

Raitas

Raitas are savoury yogurts which became important accompaniments during the Mughal rule in India. Over the centuries, a lot of time was devoted to new and innovative varieties—a tradition that continues until today.

Raitas are normally served with spiced biryanis or with stuffed breads called parathas. The yogurt cuts through the grease and spices enhancing and complimenting the primary flavors of the dish, giving it a more rounded feel.

Basic Raita

Raita

Thick yogurt	100 g/ 1/2 cup
Sugar	5 g/ 1 tsp
Salt	a pinch
Chopped coriander leaves	a pinch
Chopped mint leaves	5 g/ 1 tsp
Cucumber deseeded and chopped	5 g/ 1 tsp
Tomatoes deseeded and chopped	5 g/ 1 tsp
Chilli powder	a pinch
Roasted cumin powder (see page 19)	5 g/ 1 tsp

Whisk the yogurt with the salt, sugar, chilli powder, and cumin. Add in the rest of the ingredients. Taste. Adjust seasoning, if required. Serve chilled.

Pineapple Raita

Ananas ka Raita

Chopped pineapple	100 g/ 1/2 cup
Yogurt	400g/ 2 cups
Roasted cumin powder (see page 19)	a pinch
Red chilli powder	a pinch

Salt	to taste
Oil	10 ml/ 2 tsp
Chopped fresh chillies	2
Mustard seeds	a pinch
Curry leaves	a sprig
Chopped coriander leaves	a pinch

Whisk the yogurt in a bowl with the cumin powder, chilli powder, and salt until it is smooth. Heat the oil over medium heat. Add the chillies, mustard seeds, and curry leaves. When the seeds crackle, pour this mixture over the yogurt. Add the chopped pineapple and coriander leaves. Stir a few times until it is evenly mixed. Taste and adjust seasoning, if required. Serve chilled.

Asafoetida and Spinach Raita

Hing Palak ka Raita

Yogurt	400g/ 2 cups
Oil	10 ml/ 2 tsp
Asafoetida	5 g/ 1 tsp
Finely sliced shallots	20 g/ 1 heaping tbsp
Chopped chillies	2
Shredded spinach	40 g/ 2 heaping tbsp
Salt	to taste
Chopped coriander leaves	5 g/ 1 tsp

Whisk the yogurt until smooth and set aside.

Heat the oil in a pan, add the asafoetida and simmer on low heat until it begins to turn golden. Add the shallots and chillies and stir on low heat until the shallots are soft. Add the spinach until it wilts. Add this mixture to the yogurt along with the salt and coriander leaves. Stir until evenly mixed. Taste and adjust seasoning, if required. Serve chilled.

Spinach and Scallion Raita

Palak aur Hara Pyaaz ka Raita

Young spinach leaves, cleaned and trimmed	50 g/ ¼ cup packed tight
Chopped spring onions/ scallions	20 g/ 1 heaping tbsp
Yogurt	400g/ 2 cups
Grated ginger	10 g/ 2 tsp
Chopped fresh chillies	5 g/ 1 tsp
Roasted cumin seed powder	a pinch
Shredded mint leaves	5 g/ 1 tsp
Salt	to taste
Sugar	a pinch

Whisk the yogurt with the ginger, fresh chillies, cumin, mint, salt, and sugar. Finely shred the spinach leaves and add to the yogurt along with the scallions. Stir until evenly mixed. Taste and adjust seasonings, if necessary. Serve chilled.

Apple and Sprouted Bean Raita

Seb aur Ankurit Mung ka Raita

Finely chopped apples	100 g/ 1/2 cup
Beansprouts	250 g/ 1 1/4 cup
Yogurt	200 g/ 1 cup
Chopped ginger	10 g/ 2 tsp
Crushed roasted cumin seeds	5 g/ 1 tsp
Crushed black peppercorns	5 g/ 1 tsp
Chopped fresh chillies	5 g/ 1 tsp
Chopped coriander leaves	5 g/ 1 tsp
Salt	to taste

Mix all the ingredients in a bowl. Taste and adjust the seasonings and spices, if required. Serve chilled.

Podis and Spice Powders

A trip through the southern states of India *will* jolt your senses and waken your body from a self-imposed slumber. It is not a rude awakening; on the contrary, I never felt all my senses were being revived simultaneously. Biking through rolling hills and emerald green tea plantations was visual heaven. The scent of cardamom jostling for attention with the sweetness of cinnamon and nutmeg was ethereal.

Having a mid-life crisis means never going half measures on decisions, so I decided that the best way to travel through the country would be on a bicycle. This proved to be a boon to me and, later, to my. Slowly pedaling through the countryside much slows the pace of your travels, allowing you to enjoy more of the scenery, take in more culture, get bitten by more mosquitoes, flag and stumble about in exhaustion.Hey!....I think I veered a bit off course there.

Anyway, veering from course is exactly what landed me at Swamiji's ashram on the border of the states of Karnataka and Tamil Nadu. I had not been looking for the place, but fate sometimes intervenes to make life easier for guys in mid-life crisis.

I asked for and received shelter, but did not ask for the round of laughter I got when I thought to impress my new hosts with several yoga poses that I had learned from my earlier stay in Haridwar. I believed that I had demonstrated enough contortions to make an Olympic gymnast proud. I was obviously mistaken! Without breaking a sweat, a seven-year-old repeated all I had done, and more, as a warm up! It dawned on me that I had stumbled into a yogic concentration camp. My horror and perplexity must have shown because the Swamiji approached, laughing as he came, to tell me that this kid could do this because he had been on ashram food for his whole life.

Not surprisingly, this made me curious promoting fantasies of lunch containing huge vitamin pills or spirulina-laced concoctions designed to give the recipient unimagined strength and energy. I was greatly disappointed that lunch was plain boiled rice, ghee, and an assortment of podis (spice powder mixtures sometimes with ground legumes, beans, seeds, etc.).

Following the example of the others, I sprinkled homemade ghee onto my hot, aromatic rice and sprinkled on a bit of powder taken from the first bowl of the mixture. Wow! does not even begin to describe the assortment of sensations that swirled around my tongue and coursed through my body. I got a couple of smirks and a few raised eyebrows as I shoveled the rice in. When I was done, I was beyond caring. I ran an appreciative hand over my sated and more rounded belly and realized that I would have to take the recipe and run. Were I to stay on, I would undo all the good I had done and the one remaining occupation for me would be as a lifelong model of the Michelin man.

The powders described keep well for several months in airtight containers.

Spiced Lentil Powder

Parippu Podi

Split red lentils/ Masoor dal	200 g/ 1 cup
Split Bengal gram/ Chana dal	20 g/ 1 heaping tbsp
Split black lentils/ Udad dal	10 g/ 2 tsp
Cumin seeds	a pinch
Fenugreek seeds	a pinch
Coriander seeds	a pinch
Dried red chillies	5
Black peppercorns	5 g/ 1 tsp

Toast the ingredients individually in a dry pan and grind them together to a coarse powder in a food processor (or pound them in a mortar with a pestle). Store in an airtight container.

Blend the spice mixture with a bit of melted ghee before serving it with hot steamed rice.

Ground Sesame Seed Sprinkle

Ellu Podi

White sesame seeds	150 g/ 3/4 cup
Red chillies, stems removed	20 g/ 1 heaping tbsp
Fenugreek seeds	a pinch

Desiccated coconut	100 g/ ½ cup
Asafoetida	10 g/ 2 tsp
Cumin seeds	a pinch
Oil	10 ml/ 2 tsp
Salt	to taste

In a non-stick pan over moderate heat, toast each of the ingredients individually until they are golden. Heat the oil and gently fry these roasted ingredients until the moisture has evaporated. In a food processor, grind this mixture to a coarse powder. Add salt and store in an airtight container.

Serve with hot white rice and ghee.

Dips, Chutneys, and Pickles

Lentil and Asafoetida Dip
Mulaga Podi

Mulaga podi is more commonly referred to as gunpowder. It is an exciting concoction that combines the spice of chillies with the acidity of asafoetida and the earthiness of lentils. It is great mixed with hot white rice and ghee although it is mostly consumed as a dip when mixed with warm ghee and served with idlis (steamed rice cakes

Urad dal/ split black lentils	150 g/ 3/4 cup
Dried red chillies	40 g/ 2 heaping tbsp
Asafoetida	20 g/ 1 heaping tbsp
Salt	to taste

Individually toast the urad dal, dried red chillies, and asafoetida in a hot, dry pan until they are golden. In a food processor, grind them together with the salt to a coarse powder.

Serve as a dip with warm ghee.

Tamarind and Palm Sugar Chutney
Sonth ki Chutney

This sweet and tangy sauce is often served with coriander chutney to accompany a wide variety of savory snacks and kebabs.

Tamarind (see page 23 for preparation)	150 g/ 3/4
Palm sugar/demerara/jaggery	50 g/ ¼ cup
Dry and powdered ginger	5 g/ 1 tsp

Roasted and powdered cumin seeds (see page xxx)/jeera	5 g/ 1 tsp
Salt	20 g/ 1 heaping tbsp
Red chilli powder	a pinch

Boil 700 ml/ 3 ½ cups of water with the tamarind for half an hour. Then let the tamarind to steep in the water for an hour. When cooled, roughly mash the tamarind with your fingers and pass the mixture through a sieve to retain the pulp, but discard the seeds and fiber.

Simmer the liquid with the sugar and the rest of the ingredients, gently stirring until the sugar dissolves and the sauce is thick enough to coat the back of a spoon. Check the seasoning, if required. Adjust the consistency by adding water if the sauce is too thick. Serve chilled.

Coriander and Mint Chutney

Dhaniya Pudina ki Chutney

Coriander leaves	100 g/ 1/2 cup
Mint leaves, cleaned	100 g/ 1/2 cup
Green chillies	8
Tamarind pulp	50 g/ 1/4 cup
Sugar	a pinch
Salt	to taste

In a food processor, grind together the coriander leaves, mint leaves, green chillies, tamarind pulp, salt, sugar, and sufficient water to make a smooth, thick paste. Check and adjust seasoning, if required. Refrigerate until served.

Coriander, Mint Leaf and Yogurt Chutney

Pudina ki Chutney

This is an alternative recipe for mint chutney using yogurt to give it a tart flavor.

coriander leaves	100 g/ 1/2 cup
mint leaves	100 g/ 1/2 cup
Green chillies–	8
Whisked yogurt	50 g/ 1/4 cup
Sugar	10 g/ 2 tsp
Salt	to taste

In a food processor, grind together the coriander leaves, mint leaves, green chillies, salt, sugar, and enough water to make a smooth, thick paste. Remove to a bowl and whisk in the yogurt. Check and adjust seasoning, if required. Refrigerate until served.

Grape Chutney
Angoor ki chutney

Grapes	100 g/ ½ cup
Mustard oil	10 ml/ 2 tsp
Nigella/ Kalonji	a pinch
Chopped green chillies	5 g/ 1 tsp
Chopped ginger	a pinch
Turmeric powder	a pinch
Salt	to taste
Sugar	a pinch
Chopped mint leaves	a pinch
Chopped coriander leaves	a pinch

Wash the grapes several times to remove the must from them. Heat the oil in a pan until it smokes. Remove from heat and add the nigella. When the seeds crackle, return the pan to moderate heat, adding the grapes, chillies, ginger, turmeric, salt, and sugar. Stir a few times until the grapes begin to soften, sprinkle the mint and coriander over and stir to mix in evenly. Taste and adjust seasoning, if required. Remove from heat and serve at room temperature.

Poppy Seed Relish

Postoer Chutney

Poppy seeds	100 g/ 1/2 cup
Peeled and minced garlic	20 g/ 1 heaping tbsp
Fresh chillies	20 g/ 1 heaping tbsp
Ginger	20 g/ 1 heaping tbsp
Salt	to taste
Mustard oil	20 ml/ 1 tbsp

Cover the poppy seeds with warm water and set aside for fifteen minutes. Grind to a coarse paste along with the garlic, fresh chillies, ginger, and salt. Stir in the mustard oil. Taste and add salt, if required. This can be stored for a week to ten days under refrigeration. Usually eaten with plain boiled rice.

Spicy Mango Pickle

Raw mangoes	900 g/ 2 lbs
Mustard oil	300 ml/ 1 ½ cups
Dried red chillies	40 g/ 2 heaping tbsp
Dried ginger, ground	10 g/ 2 tsp
Sugar	125 g/ 1 tsp
Cumin powder	10 g/ 2 tsp
Turmeric powder	20 g/ 1 heaping tbsp
Salt	to taste

Wash, dry, peel, and cut the mangoes into small pieces. Break the red chillies in half. Mix the diced mango with chillies, ground ginger, mustard oil, sugar, cumin powder, turmeric powder, and salt. Place these in sterilized glass jars, cover the mouths of the jars with a muslin cloth and place them in the sun for at least a week. [We've left this recipe in place in case you live in a desert area or other sunny, dry place. Alternatively, the mangoes can be dried in the oven at 70C (140F) for about six hours until the mangoes have shrunk. Editors] At the end of this period, the mango pieces will have shrunk. Turn the bottle upside down and straight again a couple of times to ensure that the ingredients are evenly mixed. Serve when required.

Sweet Mango Pickle

Raw mangoes	900 g/ 2 lbs
Sugar	700 g/ 1 ½ lbs
Fenugreek seeds	20 g/ 1 heaping tbsp
Nigella seeds	10 g/ 2 tsp
Chilli powder	20 g/ 1 tbsp
Salt	to taste

Peel the mangoes and cut them into strips along the length of the mango. Bring 600 ml/ 3 cups of water to a boil Add the mangoes and bring back to a boil. Drain immediately, spreading the pieces on a kitchen towel to dry. Boil the sugar in 200 ml/ 1 cup of water to make syrup. Add the mango pieces. Cooking on moderate heat, stirring gently, until the mixture reaches one third of its original volume. Add the remainder of the ingredients, cooking until the syrup is thick. Cool in sterilized glass bottles. Cap and use as needed.

Mango and Raisin Chutney

Raw mangoes, peeled and shredded -	450 g/ 1 lb
Sugar	150 g/ 3/4 cup
Raisins	50 g/ 1/4 cup
Shredded ginger	40 g/ 2 heaping tbsp
Crushed red chillies	100 g/ ½ cup
White vinegar	100 ml/ ½ cup
Fennel seeds	5 g/ 1 tsp
Salt	to taste

In a pot, boil the sugar and vinegar together with 200 ml/ 1 cup of water to make a somewhat thick sugar syrup of two-string consistency. (A moderately thick sugar syrup that, when a wooden spoon is dipped and removed, and the syrup is cool enough, put a bit between your thumb and forefinger. Pulling your fingers apart, you should create two unbroken threads.) Bring the syrup to a boil. Add the raisins, ginger, red chillies, salt, and fennel seeds. Reduce the heat and let simmer for a few minutes. Add the mangoes and stir until the syrup thickens, coating the mango slices. Remove from heat and cool. Store in sterilized glass jars and serve as needed.

Fresh Chilli Pickle

Large fresh chillies	25
Mustard seeds	50 g/ 1/4 cup
Fennel seeds/ saunf	20 g/ 1 tbsp
Cumin seeds	10 g/ 2 tsp
Cloves	6 buds
Black peppercorns	5 g/ 1 tsp
Mustard oil	150 ml/ ¾ cup
Amchoor powder	20 g/ 1 heaping tbsp
Salt	to taste

Wash the chillies and pat them dry with a paper towel. Remove the tops of the chillies and hollow out the insides. Discard the seeds and stems.

In a heavy-bottomed pot, heat the mustard oil until it smokes. Remove from heat and set aside for a minute to cool. In a bowl, mix together the mustard seeds, cumin seeds, cloves, black peppercorns, and salt. Pour the hot oil over the spices until they are just covered. Let the spices steep in the hot oil for about ten minutes, then grind them to a coarse paste in a food processor. Mix the amchoor powder with this paste and set aside to cool.

When cool, stuff the paste into the chillies. Place the chillies in a sterilized glass jar and pour the rest of the oil over them. Screw the lid on tightly. Keep in a warm place for three days to macerate before using.

Pickled Ginger

Grated Ginger	250 g/ 1 1/4 cup
Carom Seeds/ Ajwain	20 g/ 1 heaping tbsp
Salt	10 g/ 2 tsp
Cumin Seeds	5 g/ 1 tsp
Red Chilli Powder	10 g/ 2 tsp
Lime Juice	300 ml/ 1 ½ cup

Combine all the ingredients and put into sterilized glass jars. Place these jars in the sun for at least five days before serving. For those of you in northerly climes, place all the ingredients in a stainless steel or glass ovenproof baking pan. (This is very important because the acid might react with other metals.) Place the tray in the oven and set the temperature to 50C/ 110*F for five hours until the ginger becomes transparent and is limp. Remove, cool, and put in sterilized glass jars.

Spicy Lemon Pickle

Nimboo ka Achaar

Lemons	300 g/ 1 ½ cup
Salt	50 g/ ¼ cup
Dried red chillies	6
Chilli powder	20 g/ 1 heaping tbsp
Turmeric	10 g/ 2 tsp
Shredded ginger	50 g/ 1/4 cup
Peeled garlic cloves	20 g/ 1 heaping tbsp
Slit green chillies	40 g/ 2 heaping tbsp
Mustard seeds	35 g/ 2 tbsp
Mustard oil	100 ml/ ½ cup
Asafoetida/ hing	5 g/ 1 tsp

Cut each lemon in half and then into quarters. Remove seeds. Mix them with the salt, turmeric, and chilli powder and keep them in the sun or in a warm place, covered, for two weeks to let the juices come out.

In a heavy-bottomed pot, heat the oil. When it smokes, remove from heat and add the mustard seeds and asafoetida. Stir continuously to prevent burning. Return to the stove at simmer. Add the garlic cloves, shredded ginger, slit green chillies, and the lemon pieces along with the juice. Simmer for about fifteen minutes, until the juices thicken and begin to coat the lemons. Cool and store in sterilized glass jars.

Desserts

Desserts have always gotten mixed press in yogic diets. Fruits and juices are considered a vital component of one's diet and certain kinds of sweets are acceptable. Although some desserts would seem too rich by present day standards, they are encouraged, because when they are eaten in moderation, they can stimulate the digestive process and impart energy.

Jalebis

Jalebis are a dessert found mostly in the north of India. Urban legend has it that invading Mughal armies brought it to India in the fifteenth century A.D. However, there is mention of Jalebis in the *Vedas* and the *Sushrut-Samitha*, medical texts written between the 4th and the 2nd centuries B.C.

White flour	50 g/ ¼ cup
Gram flour	40 g/ 2 heaping tbsp
Yogurt	20 g/ 1 heaping tbsp
Oil	15 ml/ 1 tbsp
Sugar	125 g/ 5/8 cup
Water	50 ml/ ¼ cup
Ghee	for frying
Saffron	a few strands
Crushed pistachio nuts	5 g/ 1 tsp
Juice of a half lemon	

Sift the flour and gram flour together. Heat the oil and add it to the flour. Mix the flour and oil with your fingers until it crumbles. Add the yogurt and mix well. Add sufficient water to blend the mixture to a thick batter of pouring consistency. Set aside in a cool place for about 24 hours.

Mix the sugar and water in a pot and bring it to a boil. Stir occasionally and reduce the syrup to one-string consistency (A moderately thick sugar syrup that, when a wooden spoon is dipped and removed, and the syrup is cool enough, put a bit between your thumb and forefinger. Pulling your fingers apart, you should create one unbroken threads) Add the lime juice to clarify the syrup.

Strain the syrup to remove the lime cells and any other solid matter. Add the saffron strands to the still-hot liquid.

In a shallow pan heat an inch of ghee to near smoking. Reduce the heat to moderate. Place the batter in a piping bag with a very fine nozzle. Pipe the batter directly into the hot ghee outward in spiraling concentric circles in one layer. Fry until golden and crisp on both sides. Remove from the ghee with a slotted spoon. In a receptacle large enough to hold a jalebi flat, yet small enough that the syrup will cover them, place the fried jalebis into the sugar syrup. Allow them to soak in the syrup for a few minutes. Remove from the syrup with a slotted spoon and serve them garnished with chopped pistachio nuts.

Banana Leaf-Steamed Honey Rice Cakes

Charushni

Rice	300 g/ 1 ½ cups
Cardamom	3 pods
Cinnamon	1 stick
Fennel seeds	a pinch
Coconut milk	450 ml/ 2 ¼ cups
Honey	150 g/ 3/4 cup
Raisins	40 g/ 2 heaping tbsp
Chopped cashew nuts	20 g/ 1 heaping tbsp
Salt	a pinch
Banana leaves	6

Rinse the rice until all of the starch washes away. Soak the rice in water for about ten minutes. Drain the excess water and discard it.

Bring 100 ml/ ½ cup of water to a boil with the cardamom, cinnamon, fennel, and coconut milk. Add rice. Simmer on medium heat for about twenty minutes until the liquid has been absorbed. Remove from heat and mix in the honey, raisins, nuts, and salt.

Divide the rice mixture into six even portions and place in the center of pieces of parchment paper. Fold the paper over the rice to envelope the mixture within. Secure with a toothpick.

Steam the stuffed parchment paper for fifteen minutes. Serve each packet warm.

Curdled Milk and Palm Sugar Dessert
Meetha Chenna

Milk	800 ml/ 4 cups
Lemon juice	50 ml/ ¼ cup
Ghee	10 g/ 2 tsp
Fennel seeds	a pinch
Cardamom	4 pods
Sugar	40 g/ 2 heaping tbsp

Bring the milk to a boil. Remove from heat and add the lemon juice. Stir a few times until the milk curdles. Drain through a cheesecloth and gently squeeze out remaining liquid. Discard the liquid and set the solids aside in a cool place.

Heat the ghee. Add the fennel seeds and cardamom. When the spices begin to change color, add the milk solids and sugar. Simmer on low heat, stirring continuously, until the sugar is dissolved. Taste and adjust sweetness, if required. Remove from heat. Serve chilled.

Coconut and Rice Flour Pancakes
Narial Ponna

Coconut milk	400 ml/ 2 cups
Rice flour	250 g/ 1 1/4 cup
Grated fresh or desiccated coconut	70 g/ 1/3 cup
Salt	a tiny pinch
Fennel seeds	a pinch
Ghee	20 g/ 1 heaping tbsp
Honey	50 g/ 1/4 cup

In a bowl, whisk together the coconut milk, rice flour, grated coconut, salt, and fennel seeds to create a thick batter.

Heat the ghee in a non-stick pan and spoon in some of the batter. Fry on medium heat on both sides until the pancake is evenly golden and cooked through. Continue in the same manner until all the batter has been used. Drizzle on honey. Serve warm.

Rose Petal Jam

Gulkhand

Fresh rose petals are available from most florists. You do not need expensive blooms; the petals that fall from the flowers and gather at the bottom of the basket or vase are perfect. I have cooked this recipe with marigold or lavender petals as well, with great results.

The jam is intended to be eaten in small amounts. Use it as a topping on pancakes and such.

Rose petals	200 g/ 1 cup
Honey	50 g/ ¼ cup
Cinnamon	2 sticks
Fennel seeds	a pinch
Grated lemon zest	5 g/ 1 tsp
Juice of one lemon	

Wash the petals. Boil 100 ml/ ½ cup of water in a pot with the honey, lemon juice, cinnamon, and fennel. Skim off the froth that rises to the surface. After a brief boil, stir in the rose petals and simmer until the mixture thickens and begins to become a thick gel. Stir in the lemon zest. Taste and adjust sweetness, if necessary. Remove from heat. Serve cooled.

Carrot and Reduced Milk Pudding

Carrot Payasam

Grated carrots	250 g/ 1 1/4 cup
Milk	1 litre
Cardamom	6 pods
Cinnamon	1 stick
Cashew nuts	40 g/ 2 heaping tbsp
Ghee	20 g/ 1 heaping tbsp
Chopped almonds	20 g/ 1 heaping tbsp
Raisins	20 g/ heaping 1 tbsp
Honey or sugar	200 g/ 1 cup

In a heavy-bottomed pot, along with the cinnamon and cardamom, bring the milk to a boil. Remove 200 ml/ 1 cup of milk in which to soak the cashew nuts for half an hour. Drain the cashews. Return the milk that was used for soaking. In a food processor, grind the cashews to a coarse paste and set aside. Simmer the milk until it is reduced to a third of its original volume.

Heat the ghee in a pan and fry the almonds and raisins until they become golden. Add the carrots and cook on medium heat until they are soft and all the moisture has evaporated. Add the ground cashew nuts, and honey/sugar to the reduced milk. Bring all to a boil and remove from heat. Serve chilled.

Sago and Coconut Milk Dessert

Sago Pradhaman

Sago or tapioca pearls -	100 g/ 1/2 cup
Palm sugar/jaggery/Demerara	100 g/ 1/2 cup
Coconut milk	500 ml/ 2 ½ cups
Cardamom powder	a pinch
Cinnamon sticks	1
Cloves	3 buds
Raisins	10 g/ 2 tsp
Crushed cashew nuts	10 g/ 2 tsp
Ghee	40 g/ 2 heaping tbsp
Salt	a pinch

In a pot, boil together the palm sugar, ½ litre/ 2 ½ cups of water, the cinnamon stick, and the cloves to make a moderately thick sugar syrup.

Separately boil the sago, drain, and add to the sugar syrup and continue to boil for a minute. Add the coconut milk and reduce the heat to a simmer.

In another pot, heat ghee and add the crushed cashew nuts and raisins. When they turn golden, add in the sago-sugar mixture and stir on low heat until the mixture thickens. Add the salt and cardamom powder. Stir and adjust, if necessary. Serve chilled.

Fresh Coconut Payasam

Elaneer

coconut flesh	100 g/ ½ cup
coconut water	50 ml/ ¼ cup
Jaggery/palm sugar	50 g/ 1/4 cup
Cardamom powder	a pinch
Grated dry ginger	a pinch
Salt	a pinch
Crushed pistachio nuts	5 g/ 1 tsp

In a food processor process the coconut flesh and the palm sugar. In a bowl, gently whisk the coconut water into the coconut and sugar making sure not to make it too watery.

Add the cardamom powder, dry ginger, and salt. Adjust taste, if necessary and refrigerate. Serve chilled, garnished with the crushed pistachio nuts.

Banana and Cardamom Cake

Baley Halwa

Bananas are inexpensive and plentiful in South India. They are easy to grow and maintain. The entire plant can be used for a range of domestic applications.

Ripe bananas	600 g/ 3 cups
Ghee	40 g/ 2 heaping tbsp
Fennel seeds	a pinch
Cardamom	8 pods
Sugar	70 g/ 1/3 cup

Peel the bananas and boil them in water for twenty minutes to soften them. Drain the excess water and mash the bananas.

Heat the ghee in a heavy-bottomed pot and add the fennel seeds. When the seeds crackle, add the mashed bananas and cook them on low heat, stirring continuously.

Use a mortar and pestle to pound the cardamom pods and sugar together into a coarse powder. Discard the cardamom shells and add the remaining mixture to the simmering bananas. Stirring frequently, simmer for twenty minutes until the banana mash is thick, has a sticky consistency, and one sees the ghee rising up from the sides. Pour this into an oiled tray and spread it evenly. When it cools, cut into small shapes for serving. This keeps well under refrigeration for a week to ten days.

Semolina and Milk Cake

Paal Mithai

Semolina	50 g/ 1/4 cup
Milk	500 ml/ 2 ½ cups
Cardamom	6 pods
Cinnamon	1 stick
Palm sugar/Demerara	150 g/ 3/4
Ghee	50 g/ 1/4 cup

Gently toast the semolina in a dry pan until it is golden. Set aside to cool.

In a heavy-bottomed pot, bring the milk to a boil along with the cardamom and cinnamon. Reduce the heat to a simmer and add the semolina. Stir occasionally while simmering for five minutes.

Add the sugar to the milk and continue to stir until fully dissolved.

Grease a small baking tray with some of the ghee and add the rest to the milk mixture. After twenty minutes of stirring and simmering, the milk mixture will thicken and the ghee will begin to rise to the surface. Pour this mixture into the baking tray and allow it to cool. After about fifteen minutes, cut it into small pieces and allow it to harden further in the tray. Remove and serve when ready.

This will keep well in an airtight container for up to a week.

Sweetened Broken Wheat Dessert
Lapsi

This dessert is simple and easy to prepare. Its consistency is akin to thickened porridge and is considered to be healthy and nutritious.

Broken wheat, better known as dahlia, is available at most Indian grocers.

Broken wheat/ Dhalia	200 g/ 1 cup
Ghee	40 g/ 2 heaping tbsp
Sugar	125 g/ 5/8 cup
Raisins	10 g/ 2 tsp
Broken cashew nuts	20 g/ 1 tbsp
Pistachios	10 g/ 2 tsp
Cardamom powder	5 g/ 1 tsp
Hot water	approximately 500 ml/ 2 ½ cups

Heat the ghee and add the cashew nuts, stir for a minute and add the raisins. Use a slotted spoon to remove the fruit and nuts after the cashews are golden and the raisins have puffed up. Set them aside on a paper towel to drain the excess ghee. Retain the ghee in the pan.

Reheat the pan and fry the broken wheat in the retained ghee until it is golden. Add the sugar. When it has melted, add the hot water and reduce the heat to a simmer. Stir occasionally, until the water has been absorbed and the wheat is tender. If the wheat is not sufficiently tender add water and continue to simmer. Add in the cardamom powder, fruits and nuts, and taste. Serve warm.

Lotus Seed Pudding
Phool Makhane ki Kheer

Lotus seeds/ phool makhana	150 g/ 3/4 cup
Milk	800 ml/ 4 cups
Sugar	150 g/ 3/4 cup
Cardamom pods	4
Fennel seeds	a pinch
Grated ginger	a pinch
Grated nutmeg	a pinch

Chopped cashew nuts	10 g/ 2 tsp
Raisins	10 g/ 2 tsp

Roast the lotus seeds in a pre heated oven for about ten minutes until they are golden.

Separately bring the milk to a boil in a pot and simmer it gently along with the cardamom and fennel until it has reduced to half of the original volume. Add in the sugar and ginger and bring it to a boil. Remove off the heat; add in the lotus seeds and simmer for a minute. Remove off the heat and keep aside to cool.

Stir in the nutmeg, cashew nuts and raisins and refrigerate for some time. Serve chilled.

Sweet Dumplings

Choorma Ladoos

Sugar	100 g/ 1/2 cup
Wheat flour	300 g/ 1 ½ cup
Mishri/rock or cane sugar	70 g/ 1/3 cup
Ghee	300 g/ 1 ½ cup
Chopped pistachio nuts	10 g/ 2 tsp
Chopped almonds	10 g/ 2 tsp
Raisins	5 g/ 1 tsp
Salt	a pinch
Cardamom pods, powdered	a pinch
Milk	40 ml/ 2 tbsp
Cloves powered	a pinch

Sieve the flour and sugar together. Grind the sugar and rock sugar together to a fine powder. Keep the ground sugar aside.

Mix about fifteen grams/ one tablespoon of the ghee into the flour and knead well with your fingers to get dough of crumbly texture. Add in the milk and knead to a stiff dough. Divide this mixture into even sized round balls.

Heat the ghee in a pot and fry these balls on a medium heat until they are golden. Remove with a slotted spoon and drain onto an absorbent kitchen paper towel. Keep them aside to cool.

When the fried balls have cooled down, grind them to a fine powder in a food processor.

Mix this powder along with the ground sugars, nuts, raisins, cardamom powder, clove powder and about 100gm/ ½ cup of ghee. Mix well and clump the powder in your hand to form lime sized and evenly round dumplings called ladoos. These can be stored in airtight containers for up to a month.

Sweet Semolina Dumplings

Rawa Ladoo

Semolina/ Sooji	200 g/ 1 cup
Clarified butter/ ghee	50 g/ 1/4 cup
Castor sugar -	50 g/ 1/4 cup
Cardamom powder	10 g/ 2 tsp
Raisins	20 g/ 1 tbsp
Salt	a pinch

In a pan, toast the semolina, stirring until the grains are evenly golden. Remove from heat. Add the sugar and stir well until the sugar is mostly melted and evenly mixed.

Put the ghee into a pot and heat. Add the semolina mixture along with the cardamom powder, raisins, and salt and mix until all have been incorporated. Remove from heat.

Form the mixture into round balls while still warm. Set them aside on a tray in a cool place to dry and harden (twenty minutes or more). They can be stored in an airtight container for a few days.

Pineapple Halwa

Ananas Halwa

Chopped pineapple	150 g/ 3/4 cup
Cardamom pods	3
Fennel seeds	5 g/ 1 tsp
Chopped cashew nuts	5 g/ 1 tsp
Raisins	5 g/ 1 tsp

Almond flakes	5 g/ 1 tsp
Crushed pistachios	5 g/ 1 tsp
Sugar	40 g/ 2 heaping tbsp
Ghee	10 g/ 2 tsp
Semolina	20 g/ 1 heaping tbsp

Heat the ghee in a pot and add the cardamom and fennel seeds. When the seeds splutter, add the chopped pineapple and stir rapidly over high heat. After a few minutes, when the pineapple chunks turn golden, add the sugar, nuts, raisins, and the semolina. Reduce the heat to a simmer and stir occasionally to prevent the ingredients from sticking to the bottom. Simmer for about five minutes until the dish thickens. The pineapple should be soft and chunky. Serve warm.

Saffron- and Pistachio-flavored Rabdhi

Kesar Pista Rabdhi

Whole milk	400 ml/ 2 cups
Cardamom pods	2
Sugar	40 g/ 2 heaping tbsp
Saffron strands	a pinch
Crushed pistachios	5 g/ 1 tsp
Raisins	5 g/ 1 tsp
Chopped almonds	a pinch

Boil the milk in a pot with the cardamom pods. Stir continuously to prevent it from burning and sticking to the bottom, Allow the milk to boil steadily for five minutes. Reduce the heat to a simmer. Stir occasionally until the milk reduces to a fourth of its original volume. Stir in the sugar, nuts, saffron, and raisins. Simmer for a few more minutes. Remove from the heat. Taste and adjust the sweetness, if necessary. Serve chilled.

About the Author

Zubin D'souza is Executive Chef of both the Waterstones Hotel and the Waterstones Club in Mumbai. He has chefed for more than twenty years and maintains that he is less often hired for his culinary skills as for his good looks and soothing personality (which, we, the editors, who have met him, seriously disbelieve).

Zubin grew up in one of the toughest neighborhoods in Bombay (now, of course, Mumbai) where his survival depended on his mother cooking enough tasty food to mollify the local bullies. When she finally refused to no longer cook for the small horde that came to their doorstep each day, Zubin realized that he had to get into survival mode and acquire those needed cooking skills himself.

It was love at first bite, and, as his skills grew, the number of bullies waned. No one would cross paths with an impassioned chef who had been taught to wield a knife with expertise. Giblets, anyone?

Zubin has earned several abbreviations that follow his name. He has the usual MBA and BA degrees, and a number of others, but none so valued as having attended the exclusive internship program at the Oberoi Centre for Learning and Development (OCLD) where he earned the Postgraduate Diploma in Kitchen Management. Acceptance to this exclusive program is less likely than being accepted to Harvard Law.

There is also hotel school graduation and certification from the American Hotel and Lodging Educational Institute (AHLEI) and qualification as a Certified Hotel Administrator (CHA) and (also) being a Certified Food and Beverage Executive (CFBE).

And (wearily for him), Zubin is working on his doctoral thesis on the origins of and historic influences on the Indian cuisine. This, of course, sees him traveling to remote villages and along ancient trade routes seeking to discover the secrets that he so gladly shares in his books. His thesis, when published, will reach the world at large through YBK Publishers, but until then you can catch him on his blog page, www.chefzubin.com/blog